Midland Red in Leicester

CONTENTS

PAGE 5
Introduction

CHAPTER 1 : PAGE 7
Leicester and Leicestershire Route History
1920 - 1929

CHAPTER 2 : PAGE 19
Frog Island Garage (1922 - 1927)

CHAPTER 3 : PAGE 23
Southgate Street Garage (1927 - 2009)

CHAPTER 4 : PAGE 29
Sandacre Street Garage (1937 - 1995)

CHAPTER 5 : PAGE 33
Wigston Garage (1957 - current)

CHAPTER 6 : PAGE 37
Arriva arrives (1997)

MIDLAND RED

Leicester and Leicestershire

ROUTE HISTORY

1920 - 1929

by

Peter L. Hardy.

INTRODUCTION.

To mark the half century of Midland Red operation from Leicester, I have asked Peter L. Hardy, a leading exponent of the history of road transport in the Midlands, to write a brief history of services in the County. The Company extended routes into Leicestershire during 1920, and opened a garage in the City in August, 1922, which began operating in Sept/Oct of that year. These notes, illustrating the build-up of services towards 1930, and the inception of the Road Traffic Acts, will, in due course, form part of a full history of the Midland Red Company.

J. P. ADDENBROOKE,
Divisional Manager,
Leicester.

October, 1972.

Introduction

The stimulus to produce this booklet was the fact that 2017 marks no less than four significant anniversaries associated with the Leicester operations of the Midland Red bus company:-

95th Anniversary of the first Midland Red Leicester garage opening – Frog Island on **26 August 1922**
90th Anniversary of Southgate Street garage opening **– 21 July 1927**
80th Anniversary of Sandacre Street garage opening **– 1 February 1937**
60th Anniversary of Wigston garage opening **– 5 October 1957**

In addition it is also the **20th Anniversary of the national launch of Arriva plc in November 1997**. Locally, Arriva Fox County was the successor to the original Midland Red bus company via Midland Red East (1981 – 1984) and Midland Fox (1984 – 1997).

However, our story starts much earlier when in March 1920 Midland Red managers opened discussions with Leicester Council over their bid to run services into the city. Despite there being various other applications on the table, the Watch Sub-Committee (Motor Omnibuses) decided the following May that no operating licences should be granted to any other operators unless Midland Red "with whom the Committee are in negotiation, ultimately decide not to run buses to the places to which the licences are asked for".

Most of this negotiation concerned the Committee's desire to protect not only the revenue derived from its own tramway system, but also any future right to operate motor buses. However, such was the proposed extent of Midland Red's network that garage premises were a topic of considerable importance, as this extract from a letter sent by the managing director R J Howley to the Town Clerk in August 1920 clearly shows:

"The erection of a garage at Leicester without some certainty in regard to the future of the business is a big risk. Mr Power *(O C Power, Midland Red Traffic Manager)* has I think discussed this point with you and you are no doubt fully seized with its importance."

Licences were eventually granted to Midland Red in April 1921, and on 11 May, the arrival of the first service, number 68, from Nuneaton to Leicester (The Newarke) marked the beginning of this new chapter in the company's history.

In those early days, services into Leicester, of which there were seven by May 1922, were worked by vehicles from neighbouring garages; Tamworth, Coventry and Nuneaton. But with a huge expansion planned for later in the year, suitable premises had to be found to house the growing fleet.

The growth of the Midland Red network in Leicester and Leicestershire makes for fascinating reading and we are fortunate that J P Addenbrooke, Midland Red's 'Divisional Manager - Leicester', had the foresight to commission Peter L. Hardy, a leading exponent of the history of road transport in the Midlands, to write a brief history of services in the County for the period 1920 – 1929. The result was a 15-page foolscap size duplicated document that was made available in October 1972 to mark the half century of Midland Red operation in Leicester (see opposite page).

Sadly Peter Hardy is no longer with us but we are grateful that Paul Addenbrooke has kindly given us permission to reproduce the original document in this publication and this takes up the first chapter. Over the intervening 45 years much early original material has come to light and we have taken the opportunity to use examples where we can to illustrate the original text.

Following on from this early history there is a chapter devoted to each on the four garages referred to above with the final chapter recording the arrival of Arriva in Leicester.

The authors hope you enjoy this anniversary booklet but see it as something of a 'taster' as they have tasked themselves to produce a more thorough history of 'Midland Red in Leicester and Leicestershire' over the next five years to enable publication to coincide with the centenary of that first Leicester operational base.

Our grateful thanks go to the Leicester Transport Heritage Trust, the Mike Jordan from the Transport Museum Wythall and Peter Newland, for the use of various photographs and allowing us to scan other Midland Red ephemera, and to Dave Dover, for the scan of the 1922/23 area timetable.

Andrew Bartlett and Mike Greenwood
August 2017

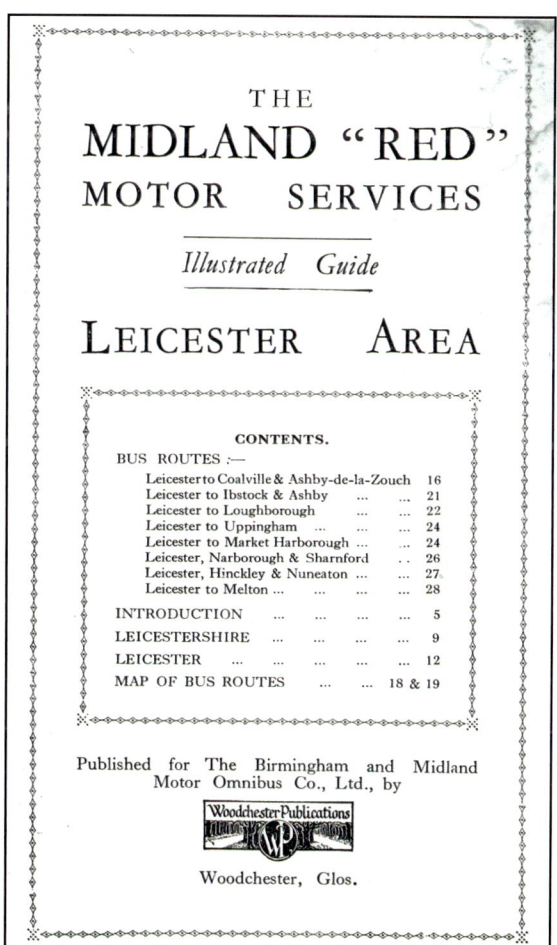

The title page of the 1923 Leicester Area Guide

Service No. **132.**—**LEICESTER AND WIGSTON (via OADBY).**

Runs to and from "The Newarkes" via the Top of Market Street, Waterloo Street, Midland Railway Station and London Road.

WEEKDAYS AND SUNDAYS.

			E	E	E		E							
			a.m.	a.m.	a.m.		a.m.	a.m.	a.m.		a.m.	p.m.	p.m.	
Leicester (Newarkes) ...	dep.		6-40	6-50	7-35	—	—	9-20	10-23	—	11-50	1-0	2-10	—
Oadby (Church)	,,	—	7-0	7-10	7-55	—	—	9-40	10-43	—	12-10	1-20	2-30	—
Wigston Magna (The Bank)	,,	—	—	7-20	—	—	8-20	9-50	10-51	—	12-20	1-30	2-38	—
South Wigston	,,	—	—	7-28	—	—	8-30	10-0	11-0	—	12-30	1-40	2-46	—
Leicester	arr.	—	—	7-50	—	—	8-50	10-20	11-20	—	12-50	2-0	3-10	—
				p.m.	p.m.		p.m.	p.m.	p.m.		p.m.	p.m.	p.m.	
Leicester (Newarkes) ...	dep.	—	—	3-20	4-50	—	5-50	7-20	8-20	—	10-20	—	—	—
Oadby (Church)	,,	—	—	3-40	5-10	—	6-10	7-40	8-40	—	10-40	—	F	—
Wigston Magna (The Bank)	,,	—	—	3-50	5-20	—	6-20	7-50	8-50	—	—	10-20	11-20	—
South Wigston	,,	—	—	4-0	5-30	—	6-30	8-0	9-0	—	—	10-28	11-28	—
Leicester	arr.	—	—	4-20	5-50	—	6-50	8-20	9-20	—	—	10-48	11-48	—

The Route from Wigston Magna to South Wigston is via Bell Street, Long Street, and Station Road.

			E	E		E	E		E					
			a.m.	a.m.		a.m.	a.m.		a.m.	a.m.		p.m.	p.m.	
Leicester (Newarkes) ...	dep.	—	—	—	—	7-50	8-35	—	9-38	11-35	—	1-5	2-5	—
South Wigston	,,	—	—	—	—	8-10	8-55	—	9-58	11-55	—	1-25	2-25	—
Wigston Magna (The Bank)	,,	—	—	—	—	8-20	9-5	—	10-6	12-5	—	1-35	2-35	—
Oadby (Church)	,,	—	7-10	8-5	—	—	9-15	—	10-15	12-15	—	1-45	2-45	—
Leicester	arr.	—	7-30	8-25	—	—	9-35	—	10-35	12-35	—	2-5	3-5	—
													F	
			p.m.	p.m.		p.m.	p.m.		p.m.	p.m.		p.m.	p.m.	
Leicester (Newarkes) ...	dep.	—	3-35	4-45	—	6-5	7-5	—	8-35	9-45	—	—	10-50	—
South Wigston	,,	—	3-55	5-5	—	6-25	7-25	—	8-55	10-10	—	—	11-10	—
Wigston Magna (The Bank)	,,	—	4-5	5-15	—	6-35	7-35	—	9-5	10-20	—	—	11-20	—
Oadby (Church)	,,	—	4-15	5-25	—	6-45	7-45	—	9-15	—	—	10-45		
Leicester	...arr.	—	4-35	5-45	—	7-5	8-5	—	9-35	—	—	11-5	—	—

E—Sundays excepted. F—Fridays, Saturdays and Sundays only.
The Route from South Wigston to Wigston Magna is via Station Road, Moat Street and Bull's Head Street.

17

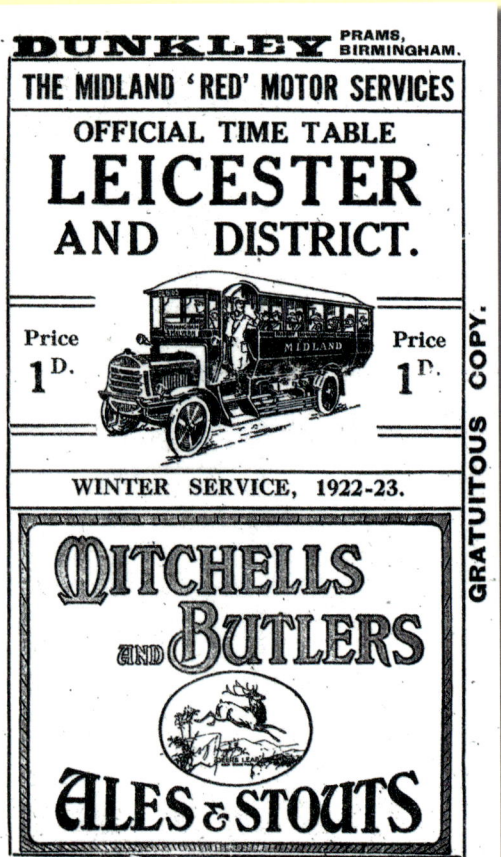

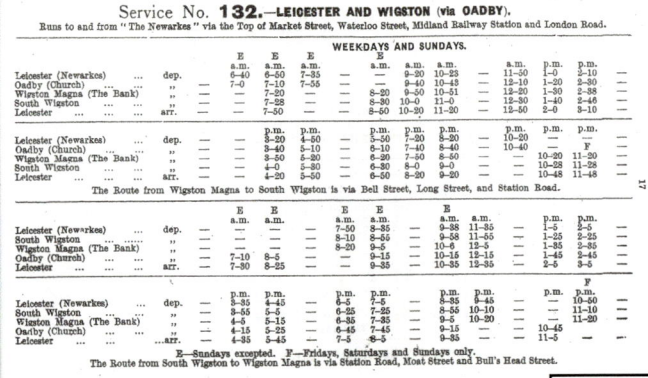

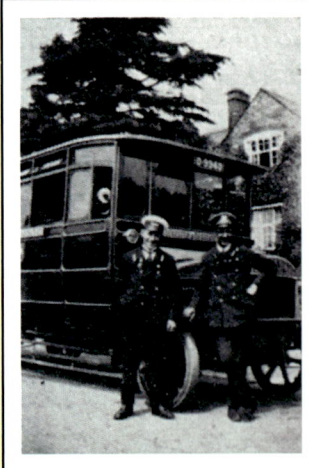

Left - This 24-page 'Official Timetable for Leicester and District' (Winter Service 1922-23) has been an exciting discovery, only coming to light in July 2017. It had been thought that prior to 1926 Midland Red only produced combined timetables covering their entire network. This timetable would suggest that marketing of networks in new areas was a key part of their business development.
Above - The timetable for Service 132 - Leicester and Wigston (via Oadby), from the booklet.
Right - Tilling-Stevens, O 9940, at Newtown Linford in the early 1920s with Driver Doncaster and Conductor B. Brumfield. The original O 9940 was a TTA2 model which was disposed of in 1919. A TS3, acquired in 1914, was rebuilt with a lengthened chassis in 1920 and fitted with a rebuilt Tilling body in 1920 and re-registered O 9940. It was further rebuilt to a 'B' type in 1926 and withdrawn 1930.

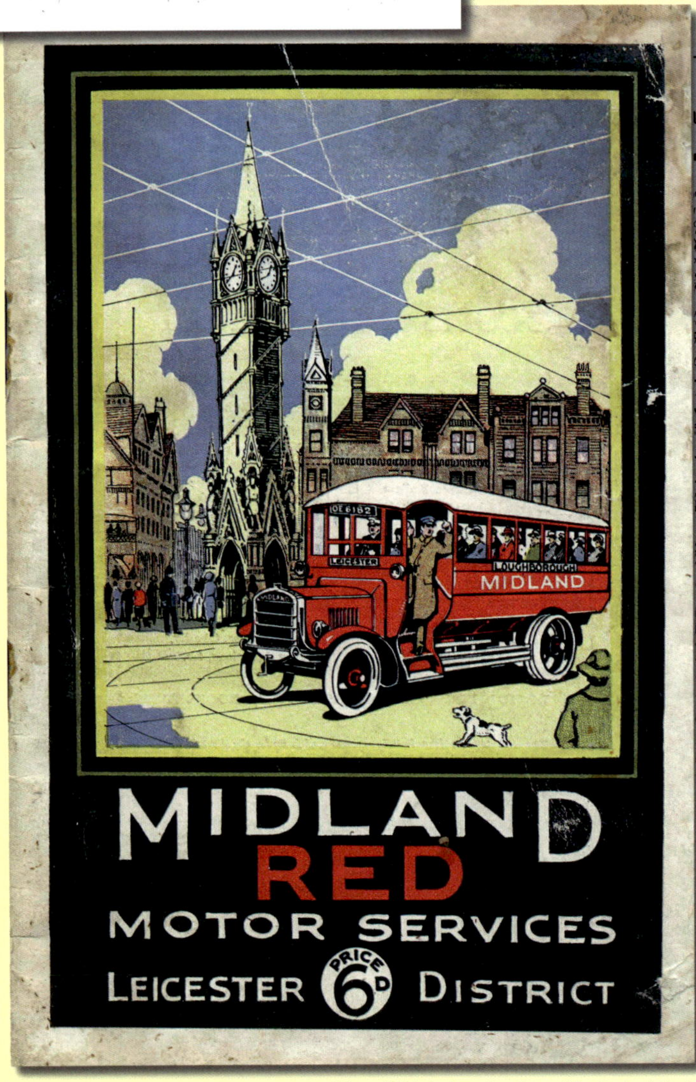

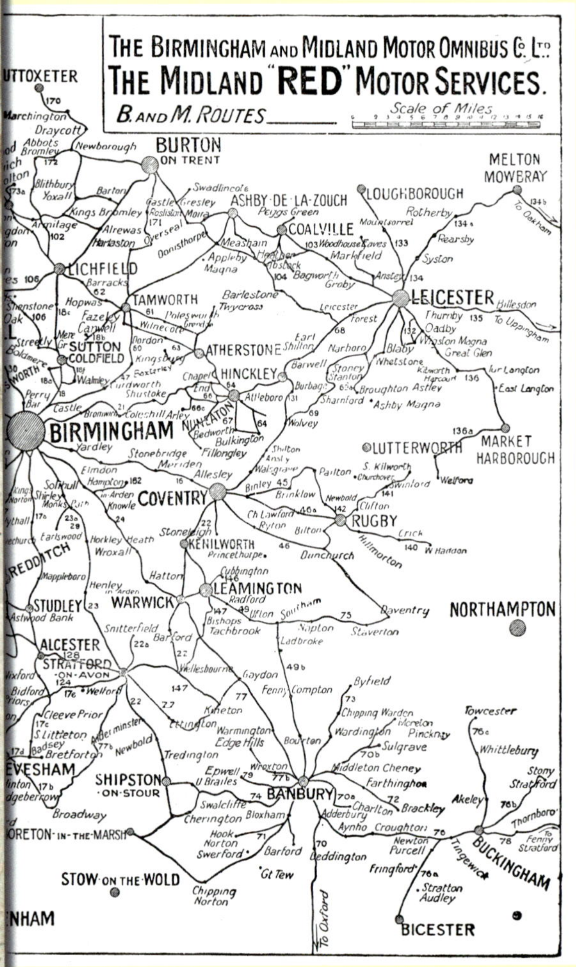

The attractive front cover of the 1923 Leicester Area Illustrated Guide and extract of the route map contained in the guide

Chapter 1

Leicester and Leicestershire Route History 1920 - 1929

(Text as used in the publication produced by the late Peter. L. Hardy in October 1972)

The move into Leicestershire and the first garage in Leicester

The first BMMO service to reach Leicester was 68, commenced as Nuneaton to Hinckley, Barwell and Earl Shilton, on 10 August 1920 and extended to Leicester (The Newarke) on 11 May 1921 (worked by Nuneaton garage). Service 69 – Coventry (Workhouse) – Leicester (Newarkes) via Walsgrave, Anstey, Shilton, Wolvey, Sharnford and Narborough – commenced on 4 June 1921 (worked by Coventry garage). This was diverted via Stoney Stanton and Huncote by November 1921, and ran only on Monday, Wednesday, Friday, Saturday and Sunday, possibly on 3 September 1921, which is when 69A commenced. This was Leicester (Newarkes) – Narborough – Cosby – Broughton Astley (Wednesday, Saturday and Sunday) and I suspect came from the Midland Motor Bus Co., Ltd., as it appears to run exactly as their service did which disappeared at the same time and carried the same reference number in the "TBR" Guide. Other Midland Motor Bus Co. services to Syston and Sileby and Mountsorrel and Loughborough went to Trent.

Service 103 (Burton – Stanton – Castle Gresley – Overseal – Moira – Ashby) commenced on 27 January 1921, and was extended via Coalville and Markfield to Leicester (Newarkes) on 15 July 1921 (worked by Tamworth garage).

Service 69B Apparently came next and appears on an old map as Leicester – Aylestone – Blaby, but by the April, 1922 timetable it has been extended via Cosby to Broughton Astley (Wednesday and Saturday).

Service 104 (Ashby – Packington – Normanton – Heather – Ibstock – Nailstone – Barlestone – Desford – Red Cow – Newarkes, operated by Tamworth on Wednesday and Saturday (most of the service from Heather only) commenced on 3 May 1922.

Raymond Tuft quotes 26 August 1922 as the opening of Frog Island, so it would be interesting to know what worked from there at first, as the main bulk of the new Leicester services did not start until September/October 1922:-

105 Newarkes – Groby – Markfield – Bardon Chapel – Ellistown – Ibstock (Daily)	**18 October 1922**
132 Newarkes – Oadby – Wigston Magna – South Wigston – Newarkes (Daily)	**23 September 1922**
Extended to Great Glen	**8 December 1923**
133 Leicester – Mountsorrel (Daily)	**11 October 1922**
Extended to Loughborough	**28 February 1923**
133A Leicester – Anstey – Newtown Linford – Roecliff Hall – Woodhouse Eaves (Daily)	**30 March 1923**
Diverted via Cropston, Swithland	**7 January 1924**
134 Leicester – Syston (Daily)	**11 October 1922**
134A Leicester – Syston – Rearsby – Rotherby – Kirby Bellars – Melton Mowbray (Tuesdays)	**31 October 1922**
134B Melton Mowbray – Burton Lazars – Leesthorpe – Langham – Oakham (Tuesdays)	**31 October 1922**
135 Leicester – Thurnby – Houghton – Billesdon – Skeffington – Tugby – East Norton – Wardley – Uppingham (Wednesday, Saturday to Uppingham. Wednesday, Saturday, Sunday to Billesdon)	**28 October 1922**
136 Leicester – Oadby – Gt Glen – Kibworth – Tur Langton - Market Harborough (Tuesday, Wednesday, Saturday, Sunday)	**28 October 1922**
136A Market Harborough – Lubenham – Husbands Bosworth – Welford (Tuesday)	**31 October 1922**
137 Leicester (Welford Place) – New Found Pool (Daily)	**8 December 1923**
138 Leicester – Glenfield – Kirby Muxloe (Daily)	**26 July 1924**

Note: Route 133A appears in the December 1922 timetable as Leicester (Jubilee St) – The Gynsills – Anstey (Daily) (actually starting 9 December 1922).

There is also a 131 service, Coventry – Hinckley – Barwell – Earl Shilton – Burbage, which was extended to Leicester, on Wednesdays, with shorts between Hinckley and Leicester, in the November 1921 timetable. This had begun as Coventry – Earl Shilton on 24 February 1921 and was diverted via Burbage on 4 June 1921. This had gone by the April 1922 timetable.

By January 1923 timetable, 134A was routed via Rearsby, Thrussington, Hoby and Asfordby and 134B via Whissendine and Langham, but the actual date is not known.

Also add 68B, Market Bosworth – Newbold Verdon – Desford – Red Cow – Leicester (Wednesday and Saturday) commenced 3 October 1923 and was operated by Nuneaton garage. A Sunday service was added by 1925.

69A was curtailed at Cosby and diverted via Enderby on 26 July 1924. Both 69A and 69B had also become Daily; 104 Wednesday, Saturday and Sunday; 132 had become virtually three routes; 135 was Monday, Wednesday, Friday, Saturday and Sunday; by the time of the first group renumbering of services, which, as far as I can estimate, was on 1 April 1925, though the new numbers do not appear in the timetable of that date.

An example of one of the types of Midland Red bus one could have travelled on in Leicester in 1923. The crew pose alongside a Tilling-Stevens TS3 chassis with a Midland Red designed 51-seat open-top body built in its own workshops in Birmingham. Note the solid wheels! In 1928 Midland Red decided to operate all its services by single-deckers and the following year several of these bodies were converted to single-deck and fitted on to a different chassis.

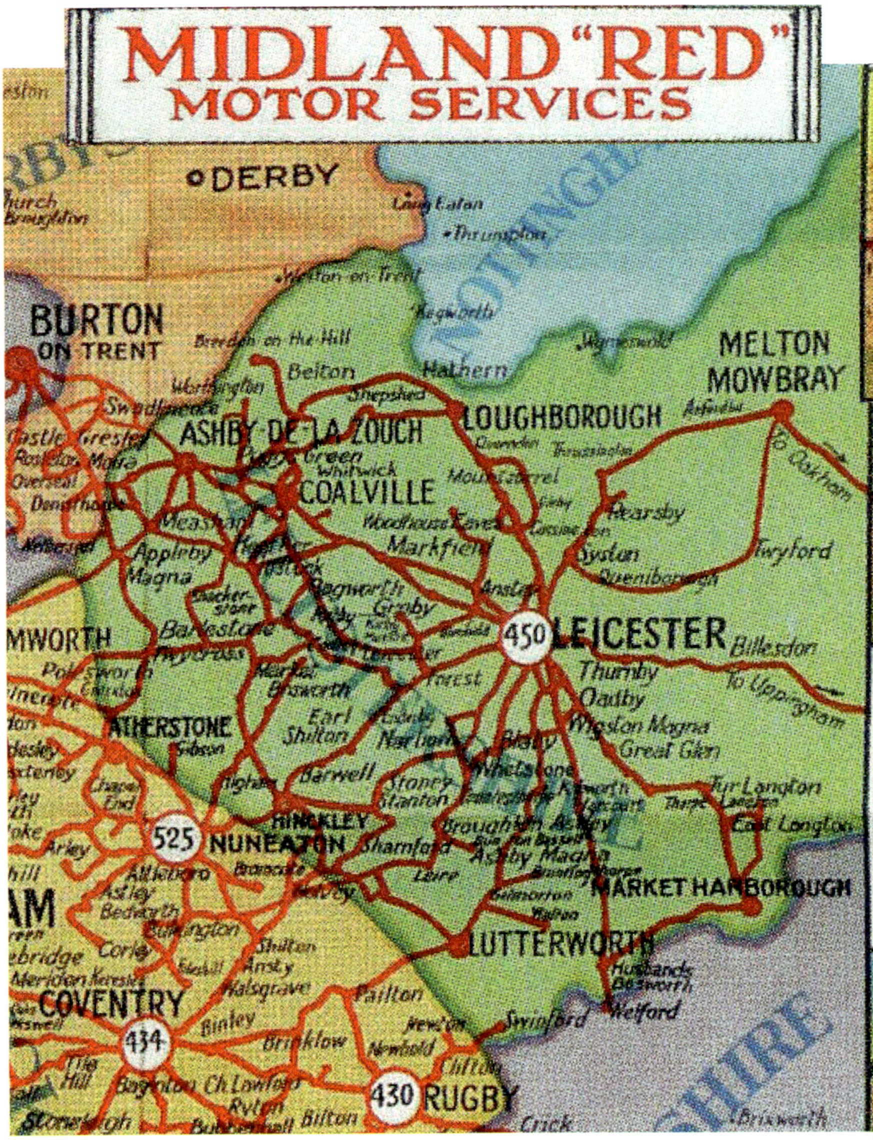

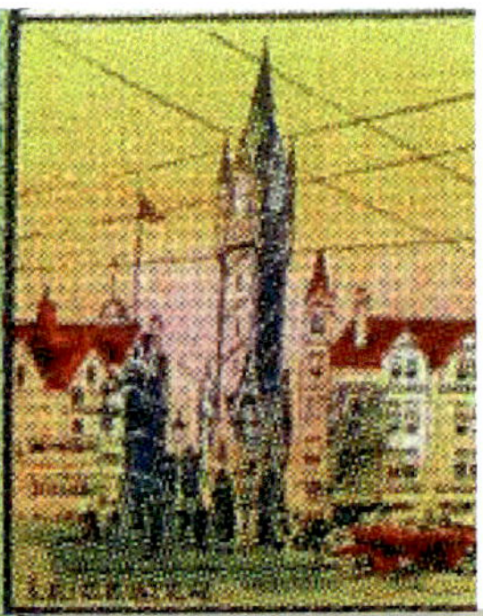

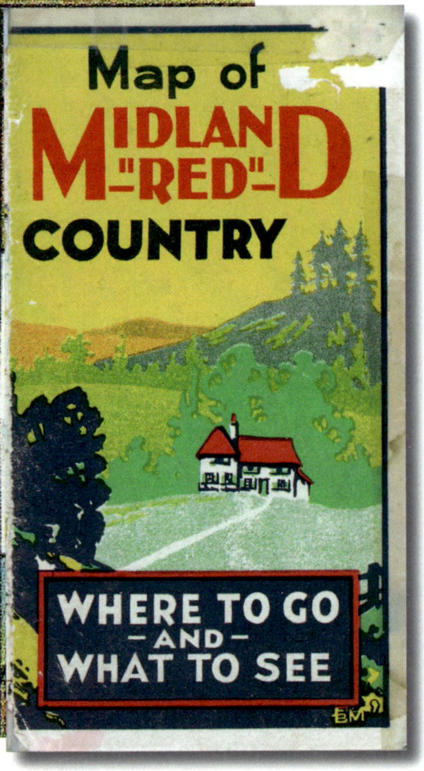

Midland Red was always keen to encourage leisure travel in order to generate additional revenue to that derived from people using local services for work purposes. To tempt potential passengers brightly coloured route maps and individual route guides were produced.

MIDLAND "RED"
MOTOR SERVICES

Route Guide—Service No. 449.

COVENTRY to LEICESTER

THE run from Coventry to Leicester is varied and interesting so far as scenery is concerned, and passes many places which have stories such as would make the fortune of a novelist in search of plots; whilst both our starting point and destination have played an enviable part in the history of the nation.

Our route lies past the old Grammar School at the corner of Hales Street, Cook Street Gate—one of the few remaining relics of the ancient fortifications of the city; Gosford Green—where a much advertised

TRINITY CHURCHYARD. COVENTRY

MIDLAND "RED"
MOTOR SERVICES.

Route Guide, Service No. 460.

LEICESTER to BILLESDON AND UPPINGHAM.

OF the making of journeys nowadays, as of the making of books, there is no end. Journeys also, like books, may be good or bad. It depends largely upon the purpose of the journey, upon the road, and upon the means of travel. Given a pleasant day, a good road, and a comfortable conveyance in the hands of competent and obliging men, a journey ceases to be a penance and becomes a pleasure.

BILLESDON MARKET PLACE

MIDLAND "RED"
MOTOR SERVICES

Route Guide—Service No. 500.

LEICESTER TO ASHBY AND BURTON.

ROBINSON came from the "most beautiful county in England." At all events, that is what he called it. He not only sang its praises tirelessly, but he sought to emphasise its glories by speaking disparagingly of the rest of the world. You know the sort of man he is. There are plenty like him.

"Take Leicestershire," he said, "Flat, tame, uninteresting. It is prosperous; granted; and fertile — in patches. But compared with —" And so on, interminably.

OLD GROBEY HALL

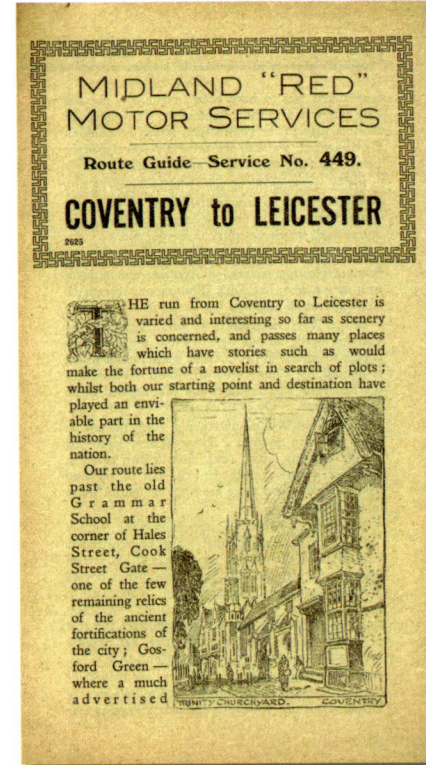

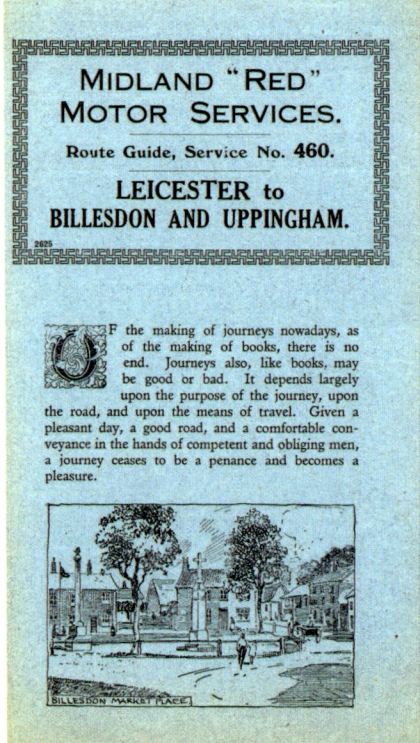

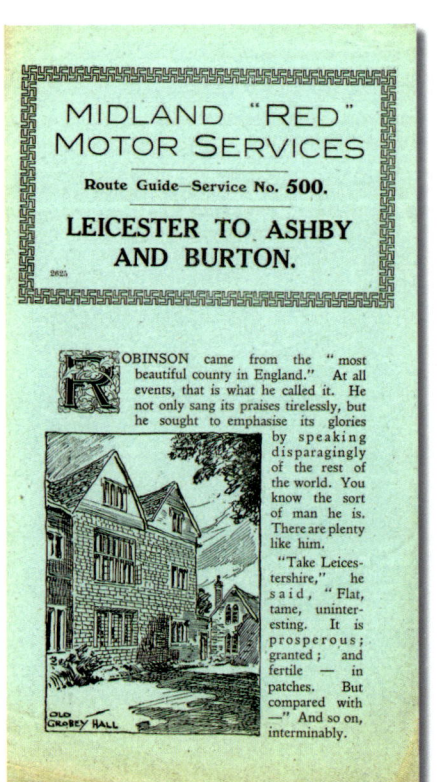

Another early acquisition, of which the date is unknown, was a firm called (according to the "TBR GUIDE") Arch Beesley & Co., operating Leicester – Oadby; Hind Hotel – Wigston Magna (Bank); and Welford Place – Wigston Magna (Bank). In the articles in the Staff Bulletin by Raymond Tuft, Divisional Superintendent at Leicester from 1928 to 1963, is a mention of a Mr. W. Beesley, who along with his brothers, operated the ABC Bus Service, the first between Leicester and Wigston and was the first of the acquired operators to work for B.M.M.O. subsequently. The service of Beesley appears in the TBR Guide at least until the end of 1923. There was also the Coalville Bus & Garage Co., running into Leicester until 1927, and presumably B.M.M.O. must have taken this service over, either by purchase or default. They ran Daimlers originally, but latterly had a fleet of Lancias. B.M.M.O. service to Coalville more than doubled between November, 1927 and May, 1928.

In **April, 1925**, B.M.M.O. services were renumbered into geographical groups. The Leicester services therefore became:

New No. | Old No. | Days operated and Route

449 69 Mondays, Wednesdays, Fridays, Saturdays and Sundays : Coventry (Greyfriar Green) – Shilton – Wolvey – Sharnford – Stoney Stanton – Huncote – Narborough – Leicester (Newarke).

450 69A Daily: Leicester (Newarke) – Enderby – Narborough – Cosby.

451 69B Daily: Leicester (Newarke) – Blaby – Whetstone – Cosby – Broughton Astley.

452 132 Daily: Leicester (Newarke) – Clarendon Park – Wigston Fields – Wigston Magna, via Welford Road.

453 132 Daily: Leicester (Hind Hotel) – Wigston Fields – Wigston Magna – South Wigston – Leicester (Newarke), via Victoria Road, Clarendon Park, Welford Road (out); also in reverse direction, out via Oxford Street, Aylestone Road, Saffron Lane.

454 132 Daily: Leicester (Newarke) – Oadby – Wigston Magna OR Great Glen, via top of Market Street, Waterloo Street, LMS Station, London Road.

456 136 Tuesdays, Wednesdays, Saturdays and Sundays: Leicester (Newarke) – Oadby – Great Glen – Kibworth – Tur Langton – Market Harborough.

457 136A Tuesdays: Market Harborough – Lubenham – Husbands Bosworth – Welford.

460 135 Mondays, Wednesdays, Fridays, Saturdays, Sundays: Leicester (Newarke) – Thurnby – Houghton – Billesdon – Skeffington – Tugby – East Norton – Belton – Wardley – Uppingham.

461 134 Daily: Leicester (Jubilee Road) – Thurmaston – Syston.

462 134A Tuesday: Leicester (Jubilee Road) – Syston – Rearsby – Thrussington – Hoby – Asfordby – Melton Mowbray.

463 134B Tuesday: Melton Mowbray – Whissendine – Langham – Oakham.

470 133 Daily: Leicester (Old Cross) – Birstall – Wanlip Turn – Rothley – Mountsorrel – Quorn – Loughborough (Cross Keys).

New No. | Old No. | Days operated and Route

473 133A Daily: Leicester (Newarke) – Anstey – Newtown Linford.

473 133A Daily: Leicester (Newarke) – Anstey – Cropston – Swithland – Woodhouse Eaves.

474 138 Daily: Leicester (Newarke) – Red Cow – Kirby Muxloe.

474 138 Daily: Leicester (Newarke) – Anstey Turn – Glenfield – Kirby Muxloe.

475 137 Daily: Leicester (Welford Place) – New Found Pool, via Newarke Street, Newarke, New Park Street, Coventry Street, Tudor Road, Battenberg Road, Pool Road, Beatrice Road, Tudor Road, Coventry Street, New Park Street, Newarke.

500 103 Daily: Leicester (Newarke) – Groby, Markfield – Coalville – Ravenstone – Ashby – Moira – Overseal – Castle Gresley – Burton (Horninglow Street).

501 105 Daily: Leicester (Newarke) – Groby – Markfield – Bardon Chapel – Ellistown – Ibstock.

502 104 Wednesday, Saturday, Sunday: Leicester (Newarke) – Red Cow – Desford – Barlestone – Nailstone – Ibstock – Heather – Normanton – Packington – Ashby.

503 68B Wednesday, Saturday, Sunday: Leicester (Newarke) – Red Cow – Desford – Newbold Verdon – Market Bosworth.

525 68 Daily: Nuneaton (Bondgate) – Hinckley – Barwell – Earl Shilton – Red Cow – Leicester (Newarke).

Note that no new numbers were allocated to old 45A (Coventry – Brinklow – Pailton – Lutterworth – Blaby – Leicester) and 131 (Coventry – Shilton – Burbage – Hinckley – Earl Shilton – Leicester) both of which had been discontinued about March, 1922.

Note the change of terminus of 133 (new 470). This originally ran from Newarke and moved to Old Cross in April, 1924, it also started from Jubilee Road for short time before this. Cross checking on other records, I find that 133 moved to Jubilee Road from Newarke on or about 1 Jan. 23; 134/134A (new 461/2) also moved to Jubilee Road from Newarke at the same time; and 134A was rerouted via Hoby and Asfordby vice Kirby Bellars.

During **1925**, changes and new services included:

461 19 September - Daily: Extended to Queniborough, and to Rearsby Wednesday, Saturday, Sunday on 9 December 1925.

471 11 April - Saturday, Sunday: **New**. Leicester (Old Cross) – Wanlip Turn – Rothley House – Cossington – Sileby – Barrow – Quorn – Loughborough (Cross Keys). Wednesday, Thursday service also from July 1925.

473 5 December - Daily: Diverted via Rothley Station, between Cropston and Swithland.

474 22 August - Daily: Extended to Ratby (via Red Cow – Daily; via Glenfield (Saturday, Sunday).

478 5 December - Tuesday, Wednesday, Saturday, Sunday: **New**. Leicester (Newarke) – Arnesby – Husbands Bosworth - Welford.

499 22 July - Daily: **New**. Leicester (Newarke) – Coalville – Coleorton – Ashby.

The BIRMINGHAM & MIDLAND MOTOR OMNIBUS CO. Ltd.

MIDLAND 'RED' MOTOR SERVICES.

Telegraphic Address: "OMNIBUS·BIRMINGHAM."

Telephone: MIDLAND 3300. BRANCH EXCHANGE.

In your reply please quote REF. OCP/LEL.

PLEASE REPLY TO The Traffic Manager. *Chief Offices:* BEARWOOD, BIRMINGHAM.

PRIVATE HIRE. SALOON BUSES & MOTOR COACHES AVAILABLE FOR WORKS & STAFF OUTINGS OF ANY SIZE OR DESCRIPTION.

When telephoning, please ask for EXTENSION No. 1.

OFFICES & GARAGES

		Tel. No.
BIRMINGHAM	11 Bull Ring	386 Cen.
	76 Lionel St. (Parcels)	6513 Cen.
	16 Seymour St. (Parcels)	3116 Cen.
	22 St. Mary St. (Stables)	2066 Edg.
	Carlyle Garage, Waterworks Rd	740 Edg.
	Digbeth (Garage)	Cen.
BANBURY	Canal Street	123 Ban.
BRIERLEY HILL, Staffs.	Harts Hill	40 Br Hill
BROMSGROVE	High Street (Office)	223 B'sgrove
	The Strand (Garage)	125 B'sgrove
COALVILLE	Ashby Road	123 Coalville
COVENTRY	6 Warwick Row Greyfriars Green	1636 Cov.
DROITWICH	12 St. Andrew's Road	43 Droitwich
HEREFORD	52 Commercial St. (Office)	1298 H'ford
	Friars Street (Garage)	2629 H'ford
KIDDERMINSTER	10 Vicar Street (Office)	108 Kidder.
	New Road (Garage)	295 Kidder.
LEAMINGTON	Old Warwick Road	184 Leam'n
LEICESTER	69 Granby St. (Office)	5275 Cen.
	Frog Island (Garage)	3414 Cen.
	Victoria Garage, Welford Road	2503 Cen.
	Southgate Street (Garage)	
NUNEATON	Coton Road	213 Nun'n
RUGBY	Railway Terrace	100 Rugby
SHREWSBURY	Ditherington	2755 S'bury
STAFFORD	3 Market Street (Office)	432 Staff.
	Newport Road (Garage)	388 Staff.
STOURBRIDGE	Foster Street	— S'bridge
SUTTON COLDFIELD	Masonic Hall Buildings	870 Sutton
TAMWORTH	Two Gates	90 Tam.
WELLINGTON	Mansell Road	167 Well.
WOLVERHAMPTON	Bilston Street	1366 W'ton
WORCESTER	East Street (Garage)	485 Worcs.
	The Cross (Parcels)	360 Worcs.

Your reference HP/DMC/B.157.

December 14th, 1927.

H. Pool Esq.,
   Asst. General Manager,
   City of Leicester Tramways &
   Motor Omnibus Dept,
     20 - 22, Humberstone Gate,
      Leicester.

Dear Mr. Pool,

Re Proposed Agreement.

     I have now seen your letter of the 7th instant.

     I am sorry I could not come over last Friday to see you, but I was away in London and I have since been suffering from rather a bad cold.

     I am expecting a message from the Chief Constable asking me to come over and see him at a very early date and I should like to keep both the appointments on the same day, to save two trips. When I hear from the Chief Constable, I will telephone you.

     If the matter is very urgent, however, I will come over specially.

     Awaiting your reply,

     I am,
     Yours faithfully,

     Cecil Power

     Traffic Manager.

A wonderful example of Midland Red letter headed paper from 1927. This letter was sent by Traffic Manager, O. Cecil Power to H. Pool, the Assistant General Manager of the City of Leicester Tramways & Motor Omnibus Department. At this time the General Manager, A.F. Lucas, was suffering with ill health and he eventually took early retirement in March 1928. We believe that the 'Proposed Agreement' related to the City's Coalpit Lane (later Braunstone Lane East) service whilst Mr. Power's meeting with the Chief Constable may be related to the new 'starting point' measures that the Hackney Carriage Department of Leicester City Police introduced in November 1927.

Changes and new services during **1926** included:

427 10 November - Daily: **New**. Leamington – Rugby – Lutterworth – Gilmorton – Countesthorpe – Leicester (Newarke).

451 15 December - Wednesday, Saturday: Extended to Dunton Bassett.

456 6 November -Tuesday, Saturday: Journeys via Great Bowden; DAILY service on route via Tur Langton.

464 9 February - Tuesday: **New**. Leicester (Jubilee Road) – Queniborough – South Croxton – Ashby Folville – Twyford – Great Dalby – Melton Mowbray.

480 15 August - Sunday: **New**. Enderby – Narborough – Blaby – Wigston – Oadby.

481 25 September - Wednesday, Saturday: **New**. Leicester (Newarke) – Broughton Astley – Leire – Frolesworth – Claybrooke Magna – Copston Magna – Wolvey - Bedworth.

500 30 January - Daily: Diverted via Woodville vice Moira, Overseal.

502 17 July - Wednesday, Saturday: Journeys extended from Barlestone to Bagworth.

504 17 July - Saturday, Sunday: Journeys between Loughborough and Coalville, via Hathern (504) extended to Leicester (merely a coupling of two routes for operational reasons).

Changes and new services during **1927**:

134 18 June - Monday, Thursday, Saturday, Sunday: **New**. Birmingham (Station Street) – Coleshill – Nuneaton – Hinckley – Leicester (Newarke).

138 16 October - Daily: **New**. Birmingham (Bull Ring) – Coventry – Leicester (Newarke) (Limited Stop).

457 by October - Saturday: Journeys between Market Harborough and Lubenham.

465 17 August - Wednesday, Saturday, Sunday: **New**. Leicester (Jubilee Road) – Queniborough – Twyford – Somerby – Oakham.

465 24 September - Tuesday, Wednesday, Saturday, Sunday: Diverted via Knossington (Tuesday service introduced 13 September).

466 13 September - Tuesday: **New**. Melton Mowbray - Knossington.

470 by April - Daily: Journeys from Leicester (Newarke).

471 by April - Daily: Increased service from Wednesday, Thursday, Saturday, Sunday.

474 15 August - Daily: Now operates to Ratby via Glenfield ONLY (see 476).

476 15 August - Daily: **New**. Leicester (Newarke) – Red Cow – Kirby Muxloe (ex-part 474).

477 20 February - Daily: **New**. Leicester (Newarke) – Stoney Stanton – Sapcote (with extension to Hinckley – Sunday).

479 15 August - Daily: **New**. Leicester (Hind Hotel) – Oadby – Great Glen – Wistow – Fleckney.

480 15 May - Sunday. Extended from Enderby, via Desford, Ratby, Glenfield, Anstey, Cropston, Rothley, Cossington, Syston, Humberstone Lane, Gipsy Lane, Humberstone and Evington, to Oadby (forming Leicester Outer Circle).

481 by October - Wednesday, Saturday: Curtailed at Claybrooke Magna.

482 15 August - Daily: **New**. Leicester (Newarke) – Blaby OR South Wigston – Countesthorpe.

483 14 September - Wednesday, Saturday, Sunday: **New**. Leicester (Newarke) – Enderby – Thurlaston – Earl Shilton - Burbage.

497 23 February - Wednesday, Saturday, Sunday: **New**. Leicester (Newarke) – Kirby Muxloe – Newtown Unthank – Botcheston – Thornton – Bagworth – Ellistown.
(Bagworth journeys discontinued Wednesday, Saturday on 502 same date).

562 9 March - Wednesday: **New**. Tamworth – Polesworth – Warton – Twycross – Congerstone – Barlestone – Newbold Verdon – Desford – Leicester (Newarke).

The various garages at Leicester were opened.

26 August 1922 **Frog Island** (Closed 20 July 1927)
22 buses

1926 **Welford Road** (Closed 20 July 1927) - 10 buses

The 1972 publication quoted a date of 1926 for the opening of Welford Road. We now know that a lease was acquired in May 1925 and from the information on the board we know that the photo above was taken in October 1925.

21 July 1927 **Southgate Street** - 100 buses

1935 **Hastings Road**, Humberstone
(Closed 31 January 1937) - 21 buses

1 February 1937 **Sandacre Street** - 70 buses

October 1957 **Wigston** - 65 buses

Also:

1 February 1918 Twogates, **Tamworth**
(Closed 2 August 1928)

21 December 1921 **Nuneaton** (Coton Road)

6 December 1925 **Coalville** (extended in 1930 and 1938) - 75 buses (after extension)

3 August 1928 Aldergate, **Tamworth** - 38 buses

June 1932 Empire Garage, **Nuneaton**
(Closed 31 December 1934)

1 January 1935 **Hinckley** - 50 buses

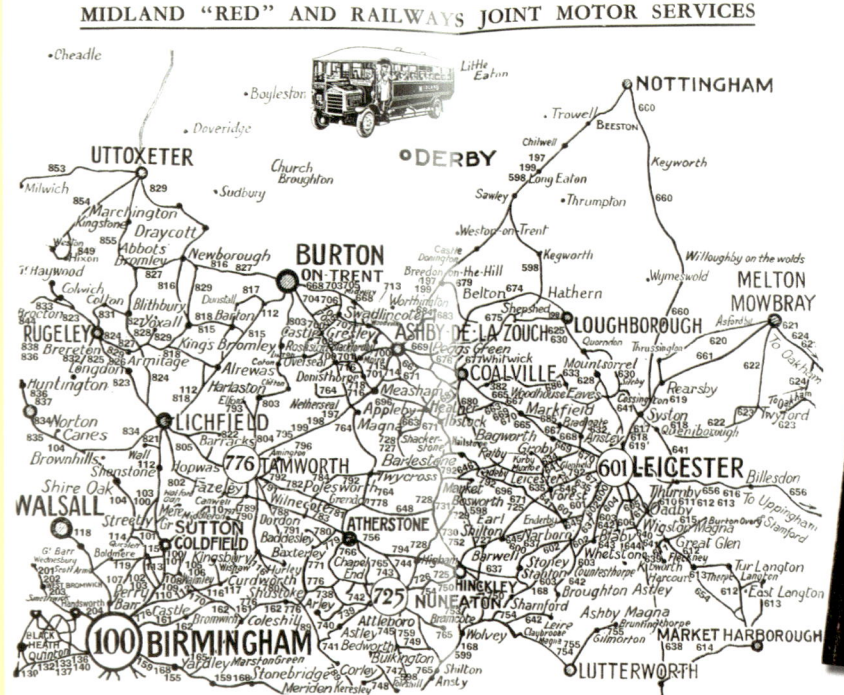

The map and cover of the 1928 Midland Red Leicester District Illustrated Guide.

Above is the cover of the 176-page Local Timetable for Leicester & Coalville dated October 8th, 1928. At right is the service 601 and 602 timetable leaflet for January 28th, 1928.

The Later Twenties and even Greater Expansion

The expansion of the B.M.M.O. company's services had been greater than had been anticipated and, by the end of 1927, some areas had already used up the allocation of numbers allotted to them in 1925. In February 1928, therefore the routes were again renumbered, allowing more numbers for each area. The Leicester services now became:

New No.	Old No.	Days operated and Route
162	134	Monday, Thursday, Saturday, Sunday: Birmingham – Nuneaton – Leicester (Newarke).
168	138	Daily: Birmingham – Coventry – Leicester (Newarke) (Limited Stop).
575	427	Wednesday: Leamington – Rugby – Leicester (Newarke).
600	449	Monday, Wednesday, Friday, Saturday, Sunday: Coventry – Stoney Stanton – Huncote – Narborough – Leicester (Newarke).
601	450	Daily: Leicester (Newarke) – Enderby.
602	450	Daily: Leicester (Newarke) – Enderby – Narborough – Cosby.
603	451	Daily: Leicester (Newarke) – Blaby – Broughton Astley.
605	452	Daily: Leicester (Newarke) – Wigston Magna via Newarke Street, Welford Road.
606	453	Daily: Leicester (Hind) – Wigston Magna – South Wigston – Leicester (Newarke) and vice versa.
610	454	Daily: Leicester (Newarke) – Oadby – Wigston Magna.
611	454	Daily: Leicester (Newarke) Oadby – Great Glen.
612	456	Daily: Leicester (Newarke) – Kibworth – Market Harborough (journeys via Gt. Bowden Tuesday, Saturday).
614	457	Tuesday, Saturday: Market Harborough – Lubenham (Tuesday, Saturday) – Welford (Tuesday).
616	460	Monday, Wednesday, Friday, Saturday, Sunday: Leicester (Newarke) – Uppingham.
617	461	Daily: Leicester (Jubilee Road) – Syston – Queniborough.
617	461	Daily: Leicester (Jubilee Road) – Syston – Rearsby (Increased from Wednesday, Saturday, Sunday).
620	462	Tuesday: Leicester (Jubilee Road) – Hoby – Asfordby – Melton Mowbray.
621	463	Tuesday: Melton Mowbray – Whissendine – Langham – Oakham.
622	464	Tuesday: Leicester (Jubilee Road) – Queniborough – Twyford – Melton Mowbray.
623	465	Tuesday, Wednesday, Saturday, Sunday: Leicester (Jubilee Road) – Twyford – Somerby – Oakham.
624	466	Tuesday: Melton Mowbray – Little Dalby – Somerby – Knossington.
626	470	Daily: Leicester (Old Cross or Newarke) – Birstall or Red Hill – Rothley – Mountsorrel – Quorn – Loughborough (Cross Keys).
629	471	Daily: Leicester (Old Cross) – Sileby – Barrow – Loughborough.
632	473	Daily: Leicester (Newarke) – Anstey – Newtown Linford.
633	473	Daily: Leicester (Newarke) – Anstey – Cropston – Rothley Station – Woodhouse Eaves.
634	474	Daily: Leicester (Newarke) – Anstey Turn – Glenfield – Ratby.
635	476	Daily: Leicester (Newarke) – Red Cow – Kirby Muxloe.
636	475	Daily: Leicester (Welford Place) – New Found Pool.
637	477	Daily: Leicester (Newarke) – Huncote – Sapcote (with extension to Hinckley – Sunday).
638	478	Tuesday, Wednesday, Saturday, Sunday: Leicester (Newarke) – Wigston – Arnesby – Husbands Bosworth (with Friday journeys to Arnesby – NEW).
639	479	Daily: Leicester (Hind) – Oadby – Great Glen – Wigston – Fleckney.
640	480	Sunday: Leicester Outer Circle.
642	481	Wednesday, Saturday: Leicester (Newarke) – Broughton Astley – Claybrooke Magna.
643	482	Daily: Leicester (Newarke) – Blaby – Countesthorpe
644	482	Daily: Leicester – South Wigston – Countesthorpe.
645	483	Wednesday, Saturday, Sunday: Leicester (Newarke) – Enderby – Thurlaston – Earl Shilton – Burbage.
646	503	Wednesday, Saturday, Sunday: Leicester (Newarke) – Red Cow – Desford – Newbold Verdon – Market Bosworth.
664	497	Daily: Leicester (Newarke) – Kirby Muxloe – Thornton – Bagworth – Ellistown.
665	500	Daily: Leicester (Newarke) – Groby – Markfield – Coalville.
667	500	Daily: Leicester (Newarke) – Coalville – Ravenstone – Ashby.
668	500	Daily: Leicester (Newarke) – Coalville – Ashby – Woodville – Midway – Burton (George Street).
669	499	Daily: Leicester (Newarke) – Coalville – Peggs Green – Coleorton – Ashby.
670	501	Daily: Leicester (Newarke) – Markfield – Bardon Chapel – Ellistown – Ibstock.
671	502	Wednesday, Saturday, Sunday: Leicester (Newarke) – Desford – Barlestone – Ibstock – Heather – Ashby (DAILY to Barlestone – NEW).
725	525	Daily: Nuneaton – Hinckley – Barwell – Earl Shilton – Leicester (Newarke).
792	562	Wednesday: Tamworth – Leicester (Newarke).

In November 1927, the Hackney Carriage Department of Leicester City Police began to tighten up their control of the motor omnibus services. The number of starting points was considerably reduced and the termini were grouped according to destination.

A colour tinted photo of HA 3630 which had a 37-seat Brush body on a Midland Red built SOS Q chassis. The 'Q' stood for 'Queen' and 110 were produced between 1926 and 1928. This example was new in 1927 and lasted until 1936. At 4 tons 4 cwt 2 qtrs they were the lightest full size buses ever built. Note how narrow the driver's cab was and the fact that the driver sat over the fuel tank. The location is Syston Memorial.

Part of the Syston timetable from the October 1928 timetable book.

Alterations for 1928 therefore include many route detail changes within the city area:

162*   by May - Monday, Thursday, Saturday, Sunday: Leicester (Western Boulevard) vice Newarke; via Braunstone Gate, Hinckley Road.
168**   by May - Daily: Leicester (Western Boulevard) vice Newarke; via Braunstone Gate, Narborough Road.
168 **   by October - Daily: IN via Narborough Road, Upperton Road; OUT as above.
575   by February - Discontinued.
599   by October - Daily: Allocated to shorts on 168 between Coventry and Leicester.
Notes:
* Also 635 646 725 and 792
** Also 600 601 602 at same dates and 637 645

603 by October - Daily: Leicester (Newarke Street) – vice Newarke; OUT via Oxford Street, Infirmary Road, Aylestone Road; IN via Aylestone Road, Welford Road.
604 by October - Daily: Allocated to shorts on 603 between Leicester and Blaby.
605 by October - Daily: Leicester (Newarke Street) – vice Newarke; OUT via Oxford Street, Infirmary Road, Welford Road; IN via Welford Road.
606 by October - Daily: Reallocated. Now Leicester (Newarke Street) – Wigston Magna – South Wigston – Leicester (Newarke Street); OUT via Oxford Street, Infirmary Road, Welford Road; IN via Saffron Lane, Aylestone Road, Welford Road.
607 by October - Daily: **New**. Leicester (Newarke Street) – South Wigston – Wigston Magna – Leicester (Newarke Street); OUT via Oxford Street, Infirmary Road, Aylestone Road, Saffron Lane; IN via Welford Road.
608 by October - Daily: **New**. Leicester (Newarke Street) – South Wigston – Wigston Magna – Leicester (Hind Hotel); OUT via Oxford Street, Infirmary Road, Aylestone Road, Saffron Lane; IN via Welford Road, Victoria Road, London Road.
609 by October - Daily: **New**. Leicester (Hind Hotel) – Wigston Magna (Central Avenue), via London Road, Victoria Road, Welford Road.
610/612 by February - Daily: Leicester (Hind Hotel) vice Newarke; via London Road, Stoneygate (vice Newarke Street, Welford Road, Marlborough Street, King Street, Wellington Street, Waterloo Street, London Road).
613 by October - Tuesday, Saturday: Allocated to journeys on 612 via Great Bowden, to Hind Hotel by February 1929.
615 30 June - Wednesday, Saturday, Sunday: **New**. Leicester (Newarke) Oadby – Great Glen – Burton Overy, via 610/612 route to London Road, Stoneygate – to Hind Hotel as 610 by February 1929.
616 by February 1929 - Monday, Wednesday, Friday, Saturday, Sunday: Leicester (Hind Hotel) vice Newarke, via London Road, Saxby Street, St. Peters Road, East Park Road, Humberstone Road, Humberstone Tram Terminus.
617 by October - Daily: Allocated to Leicester – Syston ONLY.
618 by October - Daily: Allocated to Leicester – Queniborough (ex-617).

619 by October - Daily: Allocated to Leicester – Rearsby (ex-617).
621 by October - Tuesday, Saturday, Sunday: Increased from Tuesday.
620/622/623 by May - Tuesday: Leicester (Haymarket, Humberstone Gate) vice Jubilee Road; via Wharf Street, Russell Square, Junction Road, Belgrave Road, Melton Road discontinued 18 December.
624 by October - Tuesday, Saturday, Sunday: Increased from Tuesday extended to Oakham (Tuesday, Saturday); diverted via Cold Overton (Tuesday, Saturday, Sunday); journeys from Leicester to Braunstone (Tuesday, Saturday, Sunday) – via 623 route to Knossington.
626 by October - Daily: Service numbers reallocated. 625: Leicester (Old Cross) – Loughborough, via Red Hill; 626: Leicester (Old Cross) – Loughborough, via Birstall; 627: Leicester (Newarke) – Loughborough, via Mountsorrel; 628: Leicester (Old Cross) – Loughborough, via Main Road – rerouted in City:- IN via Loughborough Road, Belgrave Road, Belgrave Gate, Jubilee Road, Bedford Street vice Belgrave Road, Junction Road, Russell Square, Bedford Street; OUT via Belgrave Gate, Belgrave Road, Loughborough Road (no change).
627 by October - Daily: IN via Loughborough Road, Belgrave Road, Abbey Park Road, Abbey Lane, Frog Island, Northgate Street, Great Central Street, St. Nicholas Street, Applegate Street, West Bridge Street, Duns Lane vice Loughborough Road .... Northgate Street, Highcross Street, Southgate Street. OUT as old inward route (no change).
629 by October - Daily (as 625/626/628).
630 by October - Daily: Allocated to shorts on 629 between Loughborough and Sileby.
631 by October - Daily: Allocated to shorts on 632/633 between Leicester and Anstey.
632/634 by October - Daily: IN via Groby Road, Woodgate, Frog Island and as 625/626/628.
633 by October - Daily: IN via Anstey Gorse, Blackbird Lane, Woodgate, Frog Island and as 625/626/628.
633 by October - Sunday: Journeys via Roecliff Camp vice Swithland, Rothley Station.
633 by February 1929: Journeys via Roecliff Camp discontinued.
636 by October - Daily: Leicester (Newarke street) vice Welford Place.
638 by October - Tuesday, Wednesday, Friday, Saturday, Sunday: Leicester (Newarke Street) (as 605).
640 14 July - Daily: Reallocated to Oadby – Enderby (Sunday); Wigston Magna – Narborough (Monday to Saturday).
641 14 July - Sunday. Allocated to Leicester Outer Circle (ex-640).
642/643 by October. Leicester (Newarke Street) vice Newarke (as 603).
644 by October - Daily: Leicester (Newarke Street) vice Newarke.
647 by October - Daily: Allocated to shorts on 608 between Leicester and South Wigston (discontinued by February 1929).

Further city area alterations that took place in 1928:

648 6 October - Wednesday, Saturday: Leicester (Western Boulevard) – Market Bosworth – Shenton – Sibson – Sheepy Magna – Atherstone (extension of 646).

650 November - Daily: **New**. Leicester (Jubilee Road) – Barkby, via Barkby Lane. Route as 617.

651 November - Daily: **New**. Leicester (Jubilee Road) – Barkby, via Syston. Route as 617.

654 1 September - Saturday: Leicester (Newarke) – Market Harborough, via Main Road. Route as 610, to Hind Hotel by February 1929.

655 by February 1929 - Daily: Allocated to shorts on 610 between Leicester and Oadby.

656 23 November - Friday: **New**. Leicester (Hind Hotel) – Uppingham – Glaston – Morcott – South Luffenham – Ketton – Tinwell – Stamford (possibly from Newarke at first).

660 1 December - Daily: **New**. Leicester (Jubilee Road) – Syston Willoughby – Keyworth – Nottingham (Queens Road).

661 1 December - Wednesday, Friday, Saturday, Sunday: **New**. Leicester (Jubilee Road) – Syston – Rearsby – Kirby Bellars – Melton Mowbray.

663 11 July - Wednesday, Saturday: **New**. Leicester (Newarke) – Ibstock – Heather – Swepstone – Newton Burgoland. Route as 632.

664 by October: Discontinued.

665 by October: Daily (as 632 route – also 667/668 and 669/70).

668 by May - Daily: Burton (George Street) vice Horninglow Street.

671 by May - Daily: Service to Barlestone. Leicester (Western Boulevard) vice Newarke (as 162).

671 by October - Daily: Allocated to Leicester – Barlestone ONLY.

672 by October - Wednesday, Saturday, Sunday: Allocated to Leicester – Barlestone – Nailstone – Ibstock (ex-part 671).

673 by October - Wednesday, Saturday, Sunday: Allocated to Leicester – Barlestone – Ibstock – Heather – Normanton – Ashby (ex-part 671).

792 by October - Wednesday, Saturday: Increased from Wednesday.

By the end of 1928 the route network has become very complex, and existed in this basic form until well into the 1960s, before political and economic dictates meant the end of many rural routes, and the increase of co-ordination in the City with the Corporation Transport Department.

Belgrave Gate Bus Station appears in timetables by October 1929 for services to the north and east, and there was movement of services between The Newarke, Newarke Street and All Saints Road, to complete the pattern of services which, from 1930 onwards were authorised by the Licensing Authorities.

New Services in 1929 were:-

614 13 August - Tuesday: Leicester (Hind) – Market Harborough (Freemasons Arms) via Kibworth, Cranoe, Hallaton, Medbourne, Weston-by-Welland, Great Bowden.

652 January - Daily: Leicester (Orchard Street) – Humberstone Lane (Railway Bridge) via Belgrave Gate and Marfitt Street.

657 25 June - Wednesday, Sunday: Leicester (All Saints Road) – Shepshed (Bull Ring) via Anstey and Ulverscroft Priory.

658 27 July - Daily: Leicester (Western Boulevard) – Coventry (Greyfriars Green) via Hinckley and Nuneaton.

659 22 June - Daily: Leicester (Jubilee Road) – Loughborough (Cross Keys) via Syston – Sileby and Barrow.

662 7 December - Daily: Leicester (Belgrave Gate) – Grantham (St. Peters Hill) via Melton Mowbray.

Other Operators

Raymond Tuft, in his memoirs in the Staff Bulletin, states that there were 95 other operators into Leicester in 1927 and lists the following. I have noted against them where I have a record of the dates of their takeover by B.M.M.O. or some other operator.

SYSTON, REARSBY, GIPSY LANE
L. H. Pole, Syston - to B.M.M.O. 1 March 1934
W. C. Smith, Syston - to B.M.M.O. 1 March 1934
F. R. Wadd, Syston (acquired from C. H. Allen by agreement) - to B.M.M.O. 1 November 1936
Godwin (later T. Weston) - to B.M.M.O. 1 December 1928
North
Moore
Thornton
Patrick

HUNGARTON
Hinks

SCRAPTOFT, BILLESDON
A. Toone, Billesdon - to B.M.M.O. 1 March 1939
Bull, Bushby - to Toone date unknown
Grey

ILLSTON
H. T. Errington, Evington - to B.M.M.O. 24 March 1937

OADBY, GREAT GLEN, FLECKNEY
A. Clarke, Oadby - to B.M.M.O. 28 December 1931
Clowes
R. H. Reeve, Fleckney - to B.M.M.O. 1 March 1936
J. C. Peberdy, Fleckney - to B.M.M.O. 12 June 1932
J. Chapman, Fleckney - to B.M.M.O. 5 January 1935
E. A. Hames, Oadby - to B.M.M.O. 1 February 1935
A. V. Simkin, Hallaton - to B.M.M.O. 1 March 1936

ARNESBY, WELFORD
W. Wallis, Shearsby - to B.M.M.O. 1 January 1931
Snutch, Arnesby - to B.M.M.O. date unknown
T. J. Miller, Welford - to B.M.M.O. 1 March 1931
W. Bond, South Kilworth - to B.M.M.O. 16 April 1932
F. W. Bromley

SOUTH WIGSTON, COUNTESTHORPE
J. Lewitt, Countesthorpe - to B.M.M.O. 25 February 1929
H. Hunt, Countesthorpe - to B.M.M.O. 25 March 1930
Chambers
A. Underwood, Jnr., S. Wigston - to B.M.M.O. 28 Mar. 1932
A. Underwood, S. Wigston - to B.M.M.O. 20 Aug. 1933

BLABY, BROUGHTON ASTLEY
F. Hall & Co., Broughton Astley - to B.M.M.O. 28 September 1931
J. W. Neale, Cosby - to B.M.M.O. 20 February 1933
J. E. & A. M. Jarratt, Blaby - to B.M.M.O. 30 May 1931
J. W. Jarratt, Blaby - to B.M.M.O. 1 October 1929

COUNTESTHORPE, DUNTON BASSETT, via Blaby
Chambers
Mrs. F. A. Hall, Dunton Bassett - to B.M.M.O. 12 April 1930

WALTON
A. C. Allen, Walton - to B.M.M.O. 24 December 1930
Cheney

ENDERBY, NARBOROUGH, CROFT
J. Clark, Narborough - to B.M.M.O. 25 March 1939
R. Phillips, Enderby - to B.M.M.O. 30 December 1935
J. A. Smith, Enderby - to B.M.M.O. 4 March 1929
R. Mould, Enderby - to B.M.M.O. 1 January 1930

SAPCOTE
Brown Bros., Sapcote - to Robinson's Burbage.
T. Haines, Huncote - to B.M.M.O. 18 March 1929

THURLASTON
Mrs. A. M. Wright, Thurlaston - to B.M.M.O. 1 October 1934

BARLESTONE
Gibson Bros., Barlestone - still operating
Deacon & Hardy, Barlestone

KIRBY MUXLOE, BAGWORTH
J. Forman, Leicester Forest East - to B.M.M.O. 26 October 1929
V. J. Wheeler, Kirby Muxloe - to B.M.M.O. 31 December 1929
Cooper
J. Liddington, Bagworth - to B.M.M.O. 4 February 1930
H. Peters, Thornton - to B.M.M.O. 30 September 1930

GLENFIELD, RATBY
Astill & Jordan, Ratby - still operating
Hylton & Dawson, Glenfield - still operating
C. S. Peach, Glenfield - to B.M.M.O. 11 June 1932
L. Wood, Ratby - to B.M.M.O. 20 February 1933
J. W. Jordan, Ratby - to B.M.M.O. 1 July 1932

GROBY, MARKFIELD, COALVILLE
T. H. Smith, Groby - to B.M.M.O. 16 August 1954
W. D. Warner, Markfield
L. D. Brown, Markfield - to B.M.M.O. 16 March 1963
A. W. Whetton, Coalville - to B.M.M.O. 27 June 1932
St. Saviours - to B.M.M.O. 26 October 1929
Red Rambler
J. Moore, Whitwick - to B.M.M.O. 25 March 1932
Smith, Stanton
Hamblin, Groby - to B.M.M.O. date unknown
Carrington
C. W. Shaw, Coalville - to B.M.M.O. 1 March 1937

IBSTOCK
H. Bircher, Ibstock - to B.M.M.O. 6 June 1932
Windridge, Sons & Riley
A. R. Hipwell, Ibstock - to L. D. Brown date unknown
Black
H. & A. Saunt, Ellistown - to B.M.M.O. 31 December 1938

ANSTEY, BRADGATE
C. W. Moore, Anstey - to B.M.M.O. 29 March 1929
Mason, Anstey - to Leicester & District and C. H. Allen, date unknown.
J. H. Hutton, Anstey - to B.M.M.O. 1 April 1944

WOODHOUSE
Leicester & District - to C. H. Allen 1 Nov. 1936 (by arrangement with B.M.M.O.) - to B.M.M.O. 30 July 1955
C. H. Allen, Mountsorrel - to B.M.M.O. 30 July 1955
Prestwells, Woodhouse Eaves - to B.M.M.O.

BIRSTALL, LOUGHBOROUGH
Leicester & District - to Soar Valley 1 Nov. 1936 (by arrangement with B.M.M.O.) - to B.M.M.O. 30 July 1955
C. H. Allen, Mountsorrel - to B.M.M.O. 30 July 1955
Kemp & Shaw, Leicester - to B.M.M.O. 30 July 1955 (operated as subsidiary until 1 January, 1959)
H. Boyer, Rothley - to B.M.M.O. 1 February 1959
W. Housden, Loughborough
J. H. Squire, Rothley - to B.M.M.O. 25 March 1931
Branston (Eclipse) - to Kemp & Shaw, 1934
Howlett, Quorn - still operating

SILEBY
J. Squires - to B.M.M.O. 25 November 1935 (transferred to Trent - 2 January 1938)
Hayward
Harris
E. W. Bott, Sileby

HINCKLEY
Leicester & District - to B.M.M.O. 1 November 1936
G. W. Woodward, Barwell - to B.M.M.O. 25 March 1930

There is no mention above of F. Preston, Kirkby Mallory (to B.M.M.O. 24 June 1931); Highfield Motor Services (How), Leicester (to B.M.M.O. 1 Jan. 1932); J. Bland, Grantham (to B.M.M.O./Lincs. 1 May, 1932); C. W. Bishop, Asfordby (to B.M.M.O. 25 March 1934); J. E. Ball, Hugglescote (to B.M.M.O. 21 May 1936); H. Fowkes, Ibstock (to B.M.M.O. 25 Sept. 1936).

Highfields did not start until October, 1927 (Leicester – Birmingham), Bland was even later than that, and it may be that some of the others were also late starters, or were considered to be mainly operators to other places (Ball and Fowkes to Coalville; Bishop to Melton Mowbray; Bland to Grantham).

Elsewhere in his articles, are mentions of Liversedge and Ward as two other operators on Syston, also "Ecstasy" and "X Service" on Leicester – Hinckley.

In view of the activities of the Leicester City Police in 1927, it seems to be very unlikely that any **new** service of reasonable importance or frequency was started after this, so that most of the B.M.M.O. main services started after this date were taken over from other operators. B.M.M.O. did not start on Hungarton and Beeby until 1 January 1930, and I would suggest that this is the take over of Hinks (above) who is otherwise not accounted for. When B.M.M.O. started Countesthorpe on 15 August, 1927, they ran via Blaby and S. Wigston from the start (note the operator Chambers not accounted for did this also). I have no exact starting dates for Barkby and Humberstone Lane other than the month (November, 1928 and January, 1929).

Co-ordination agreements with local operators:-
13 July 1931 - Leicester & District (Leicester – Hinckley).
17 August 1931 - W.C. Smith, L. Pole, F.R. Wadd (Leicester – Syston).
28 September 1931 - Gibson Bros. (Leicester – Desford).
28 September 1931 - C.H. Allen, Leicester & District, H. Boyer, Kemp & Shaw (Leicester – Loughborough)
12 January 1932 - F.R. Wadd (Leicester – Melton, via Twyford – Tuesdays only)
9 May 1932 - Brown Bros., Sapcote; J Clark, Narborough (Leicester- Sapcote)
9 May 1932 - R. Phillips, Enderby; J. Clark, Narborough; Brown Bros., Sapcote; Mrs Wright, Thurlaston (Leicester – Enderby – Narborough – Cosby)
October 1932 - E.W. Farrow, Melton Mowbray; M. King, Long Clawson (Melton – Oakham, via Whissendine)

The Birmingham and Midland Motor Omnibus Co., Limited.

RULES AND REGULATIONS.

The Company will make every effort to maintain the services enumerated in this Guide, but they give no guarantee that same shall be performed and they reserve the right to alter, suspend, or withdraw the running of any Vehicle or Service without notice of any description. They will not be liable for any loss, damage, injury, or inconvenience that any passenger may sustain for any failure to maintain the same, or for want of punctuality in the Service.

(1)—Passengers are cautioned not to enter or alight from the Omnibuses while the vehicles are in motion.

(2)—Passengers are requested to hail the driver when they wish the Omnibus to stop for them to enter.

(3)—Passengers are earnestly requested, on paying the correct fare, to see that they receive a ticket corresponding with the amount paid, properly punched in the section in which they enter the vehicle, and to retain the ticket, and to produce it when requested to by the Company's officials. Passengers are reminded that they are liable to pay the fare whether they are requested to by the Conductor or not.

Children between 5 and 14 years of age, if not occupying a seat, can travel at HALF-PRICE, as per schedule herewith.

1d., 1½d., or 2d. Fare	Children	1d.	1/3 or 1/4 Fare	Children	8d.
2½d., 3d., 3½d., or 4d. Fare	,,	2d.	1/5 or 1/6	,,	9d.
4½d., 5d., 5½d., or 6d. ,,	,,	3d.	1/7 or 1/8	,,	10d.
6½d., 7d., 7½d., or 8d. ,,	,,	4d.	1/9 or 1/10	,,	11d.
9d. or 10d.	,,	5d.	1/11 or 2/-	,,	1/-
11d. or 1/-	,,	6d.	2/1 or 2/2	,,	1/1
1/1 or 1/2	,,	7d.	2/3 or 2/4	,,	1/2

Children under FIVE years of age FREE if not occupying a seat, providing that not more than one such child accompanies any passenger. Additional children, irrespective of age, MUST BE PAID FOR.

The Company reserve the right to increase Fares on any route without notice.

DOGS. Small dogs may be carried at the owner's risk, if they are clean and are not a nuisance or cause inconvenience to other passengers, and provided there is sufficient accommodation to carry them conveniently. RATES—6d. stage or under, 1d.; over 6d. and under 1/-, 2d.; over 1/- and not exceeding 2/-, 3d.; and an additional 1d. for each 1/- or portion thereof paid by a single passenger for the same journey. The Company, however, reserve the right to refuse any dog.

STOPPING PLACES.—Omnibuses will STOP ANYWHERE (IN REASON) to pick up or set down passengers.

PASSENGERS' LUGGAGE AND PARCELS.

Passengers' luggage and parcels will be carried in the Omnibuses when there is sufficient accommodation available. Accompanied luggage and parcels are only carried at owner's risk, and under the Conditions and Rates given below:—

CONDITIONS.

(1)—Luggage or Parcels up to 21-lbs. in weight, the dimensions of which do not exceed 20″ × 10″, will be carried Free; all Luggage or Parcels, exceeding the dimensions given above, must be paid for, irrespective of weight.

(2)—The Company reserve the right to refuse to carry any package, parcel, or luggage.

RATES.

21-lbs. and up to 35-lbs. ... 2d. | 35-lbs. and up to 56-lbs. ... 4d.

Greater Weights than 56-lbs. will be charged *pro rata*.

Passengers are advised to send heavier luggage and packages by the Company's Commercial Road Motor Service.

Passengers should obtain tickets for all amounts paid for luggage, &c.

N.B.—Bicycles, Perambulators, large Mail Carts, &c., cannot be carried in or on any Omnibus at any time.

COMPLAINTS.

Any complaint as to any irregularity in the Service or incivility on the part of the Company's employees should be reported in writing to—

Chief Offices—
547, Bearwood Rd., Smethwick.
Telephone, 2577 Midland
City Office—11, Bull Ring.
Telephone : 386 Central.
Local Garage : Frog Island Leicester Tel. 3414 Central.

O. C. POWER, Traffic Manager.

The 'Rules and Regulations' from the Winter 1922-23 timetable book

Father's days on the buses

SEEING the report in the Mercury on the fire at the Martins Dyers and Frisby Jarvis factory on Frog Island, brought back a few memories for M Halford, of Leicester.

M Halford writes: "My father, Richard William Halford, better known as Bill, was one of the first bus drivers to start in Leicester (this was about 1920-21) for the Birmingham and Midland Motor Omnibus Company (later known as Midland Red) and this building yard was used for the few buses they had at the time before the Southgate and Sandiacre garages were built.

CAREER: Mr Bill Halford

"The buses were small and not very high and I can remember the small arch gateway the buses used to squeeze through.

"My father told me he was about 22 years old when he was transferred from Birmingham to Leicester. He told me buses were often brought to his 'digs' which were on a street where the maternity hospital is now, off Oxford Street.

"During the war years he drove troops to many parts of the country and after the war was over he took Leicester City players to away matches and finally ended up one of the main coach tour holiday drivers (very rare in those days)."

HA 2376 was a Standard SOS (Tilling) of 1924 with locally built Brush of Loughborough 32 seat bodywork, photographed at the terminus in Syston. The bus was withdrawn in 1934.

Leicester Mercury - 11th May 2005

Chapter 2

Frog Island Garage (1922 - 1927)

The company leased premises at Frog Island, seen in the photo on the right directly below Frisby & Jarvis's factory. Frog Island garage was opened on 26 August 1922. It could hold 30 vehicles, although the initial allocation was eight Tilling Stevens TS3s, seven saloons and one charabanc. Within a year this had risen to 22, and by 1925, it was so overcrowded that a temporary garage on Welford Road, was rented.

A rare view of the interior of the Frog Island premises, taken around 1926. There are still some TS3s to be seen, but these were increasingly being replaced by the company's own "Standard SOS" saloons that were better suited to taking on the competition. The fourth vehicle from the front in the left hand row is a Tilling-Stevens 'FS' open-top double-decker. It is said that there were almost 100 proprietors operating almost 400 vehicles on Midland Red routes in Leicestershire by the end of the 1920s.

A closer look at the interior of Frog Island garage from April 1927, while its fleet was hard at work. Staff notices are displayed on the board on the left at the rear, and the bicycles on the wall to the right reflect the mode of transport some drivers, conductors and maintenance staff used to get to and from work. There is a prominent "SMOKING NOT ALLOWED" sign, though nothing to show the speed limit within the garage, which would have been 5 mph or less.

Frog Island closed at the end of business on 20 July 1927; the next day, the new premises at Southgate Street became operational.

Raymond Tuft

We are very fortunate that Midland Red employed Raymond Tuft, who came to Leicester in April 1928, becoming Divisional Traffic Superintendent in April 1930. He became synonymous with Midland Red in Leicester and was known locally as Leicester's "Mr Transport". He retired in 1963.

In 1956 and 1957 his memoirs were published in eleven instalments in the Midland Red Staff Bulletin, creating some further correspondence and shorter articles later on. His writing is like a very good novel; a sound story, engaging characters, fascinating detail, amusing and tragic incidents all told in a very readable style. One of the pleasures of such an autobiography is to begin to feel that you know the author, fitting together all the clues until the full picture emerges.

As a schoolboy Raymond Tuft was fascinated by trams and tramlines and at the age of sixteen in January 1913 he obtained a clerical post at Walsall Corporation Tramways, working in various offices. In August 1915 he moved to BET (British Electric Traction) at the Darlaston depot of South Staffordshire Tramways as a wages clerk, remaining with this concern until the tramways closed at the end of March 1924.

This event prompted the move to Midland Red, at first as a conductor on the Birmingham to Walsall service, but he was soon taking up an Inspector post at Nuneaton. He was to return there, after a spell in the Black Country and in the timetable office at Bearwood, as Resident Inspector in February 1925. In July 1927 Mr Tuft returned to the timetable office at Bearwood and was then "posted to Leicester", at Easter 1928, where he would remain for 35 years!

Here is what Raymond Tuft had to say about Frog Island in "Raymond Remembers".

THE "FROG-ISLAND" FRATERNITY

Good buses, good Inspectors, envisage good Conductors and Drivers, and at Leicester "He was at Frog Island" signifies experience with a standard of ability to be emulated by others. Quite a number of men have passed on, or retired, but we still have some of the original band, who must be secretly amused at the changed times. I have mentioned Mr. F. T. Shepherd and Mr. J. A. Marshall; then there were: Conductor W. J. Kenderdine, now Divisional Staff Officer; W. E. V. Hunt, now Conductors' Training Instructor; J. Edmands, now Traffic Superintendent, Sandacre; B. Brumfield, now Travelling Inspector; Mr. J. Knight, now Engineering Superintendent, Southgate Street; Mr. L. J. Ayres, now Engineering Foreman, Southgate Street; Mr. S. Morris, now Engineering Foreman, Southgate Street; Mr. A. Jones, now Engineering Garage Hand, Southgate Street; Driver W. H. Rogers, now Garage Traffic Assistant, Southgate Street; H. Dean, now of the Lost Property and Private Hire Department, Peacock Lane; B. S. Blin-Stoyle, now Garage Traffic Assistant, Southgate Street; Driver H. Kinder, T. Laundon, J. W. Dean and G. Law, all serving at Southgate Street; Conductor E. Boot and G. Jarvis, also at Southgate Street. Incidentally, Conductor Boot used to work on Sileby and will recall having Mr. R. Brandon (now Traffic Manager) as his "Learner" in 1927.

It would require a separate narrative to do justice to Mr. J. A. Marshall—"Gaffer Marshall" as he was called. His personal memoirs, and his impact upon our Company at the right time, would make interesting reading. Like his colleague—Mr. J. Knight —he was an engineer "raised in steam"—which according to Kipling's "McAndrew," is the only motive power worth mentioning! I do know that he kept us out of our beds many a night, regaling us with tales of seafaring, engineering (including boiler engineering), pigeon shooting, ditched buses and the standard tackle for such breakdowns, etc. An abridged story like mine cannot adequately cope with the matter.

STRATEGY—AND TACTICS

In those days we wanted men who could be relied upon to take steps to safeguard the traffic which should rightly fall to their buses—and not lightly suffer the disappointment or discouragement of seeing another bus pulling away from each salient point just as they arrived. We had such drivers and conductors; in fact, other proprietors offered some of them an additional £1 per week to go and work for them. The great thing was, not to speed about the roads, run just a little late, look up the entries, the side streets, side lanes, and look to the rear. Some of the other proprietors on the Syston route used to have our times posted on their windscreens in front of them so that they could run in front at every opportunity. We used to be up at Canal Street at 7.15 a.m. most mornings to watch operations.

We have in the office a Syston timetable dated December 9th, 1922, which shows eight journeys per day on Mondays to Fridays, twelve on Saturdays and seven on Sundays. Today there are 122 journeys per day on Mondays to Fridays, 144 on Saturdays, and 68 on Sundays! Each main service had its quota of five other proprietors and, of course, we were in a minority, very much so in places. However, from the end of 1927, the strain of keeping-up with the "Leicester Conditions" began to tell on the weaker of the firms; the "Out Private" was a big expense, a big penalty for hanging back on to another proprietor's time. We "covered the service" by another bus, and nonplussed the other proprietors on occasions—who had thought we should miss our stand in Leicester. But it would take too long to go into these operations.

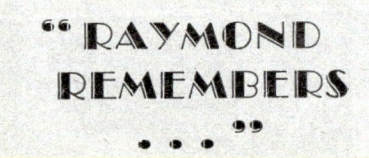

LICENCES GRANTED BY THE LEICESTER CITY COUNCIL WATCH COMMITTEE

	New Licences	Renewals
20 June 1922		
Omnibuses	20	
Omnibus drivers	25	11
Omnibus conductors	8	2
5 September 1922		
Omnibuses	21	
Omnibus drivers	34	9
Omnibus conductors	17	5
	New Licences	Renewals
14 November 1922		
Omnibuses	15	
Omnibus drivers	15	1
Omnibus conductors	6	2

Whilst it is acknowledged that there were numerous operators working into Leicester at this time, the dates would suggest that the majority of the new licences issued were probably to Midland Red men.

The authors checked the local papers of late 1922 period but it would appear that the arrival of Midland Red in the city was not considered newsworthy. However, there was quite a lot of correspondence relating to Midland Red in August 1923.

'BUS SERVICES.

Open Letter to Town Clerk and Chief Constable.

Sirs,—Some two years ago, upon the application of the Midland Red 'Bus Company for running powers in Leicester, after many interviews and deliberations an agreement was drawn up and approved by the Chief Constable and Watch Committee that power be granted to the 'Bus Company in preference and in opposition to the then services being run by local and county firms. Arrangements and sanction were given for two 'buses only to stand in the Newarke at the same time.

It was also agreed that the 'Bus Company be not allowed to pick up or set down passengers between the Newarke and the tram termini of the city in opposition to the local tram service, otherwise they were to charge the tram fare extra for each passenger. Were the extra fares handed over to the tramway management for the benefit of the rates?

You (the Town Clerk and Chief Constable) are aware that the agreement drawn up by yourselves on behalf of the City Council would not hold water. Instead of two 'buses a matter of six or eight are often left standing in the Newarke monopolising and endangering the safety of the public, and frequently holding up the traffic.

Local firms applied for this position previous to the Red 'Bus Company, but were refused. Are you aware that before permission should have been granted the full facts should have been placed before the City Council and an application made for the Newarke to be proclaimed a public stand and should have been advertised accordingly to fulfil the requirements of the Ministry of Transport, also to enable any resident in that locality to raise any objection if they so desired?

As public servants of this city you should be aware that complaints have frequently been made against granting running facilities to outside firms in preference to members of the local Association. Red 'Buses are allowed to stand in the Newarke for hours at a time opposite the Technical School, while other 'bus owners are barely allowed to pick up passengers, and are soon hounded by the police.

Only last week the Red 'Buses were allowed to overload in the presence of the police at Humberstone Gate to convey passengers to Market Bosworth Show, while other local coaches were waiting to pick up for the same destination at the same fare.

You are highly-paid servants of the local ratepayers, and it is your duty to safeguard their trade interests, and they should be your first consideration.—Yours faithfully,

WALTER E. STURGESS, F.I.M.T.,
Chairman, Leicester and District Motor Coach Owners' Association and Motor Trades Association.

Mail Aug. 16th 1923.

One assumes that this was the same Walter E. Sturgess who became a prestige car dealer. He must have forgiven the 'Red' because later timetables carried his adverts!

The former Frog Island garage photographed on 11 August 2009.

The premises were put to a variety of uses after 1927, including a motor workshop and tyre depot. However, a huge fire which broke out on the night of 30 November 2015 virtually destroyed the building, which is seen here at the beginning of December 2015, just prior to the start of demolition work. The photo at the bottom of the page appeared in the Leicester Mercury on 1 December 2015, and shows the blaze at its height.

It is Thursday 10 March 1927, and building work at the new Southgate Street garage is proceeding, though perhaps not at a particularly fast rate. Two workmen survey the scene from the scaffolding above what will become the iconic "Midland" entrance on Peacock Lane (see below), while a third bowler-hatted gentleman (who we might guess is the foreman) stands in the depths of the garage. Modern-day Health and Safety rules are conspicuous by their absence. Opening day – 21 July – is exactly 19 weeks away.

A three storey office block was built at 12 Peacock Lane, next door to the garage. The Peacock Lane entrance was a splendid affair, framed by brickwork pillars topped with a stone beam on which the word "Midland" was inscribed.

Chapter 3

Southgate Street Garage
(1927 - 2009)
Garage Identification Code: SS

With Midland Red continuing to expand its operations in Leicestershire, the search for a new garage to replace the existing, overcrowded premises took on greater importance, particularly as the lease on Welford Road was only ever intended to be short-term.

A large corner site covering almost 6,250 square metres was acquired on the junction of Southgate Street and Peacock Lane. It is clearly marked on the 1930 Ordnance Survey map below. Remains of a Roman pavement were discovered during the excavation of an inspection pit.

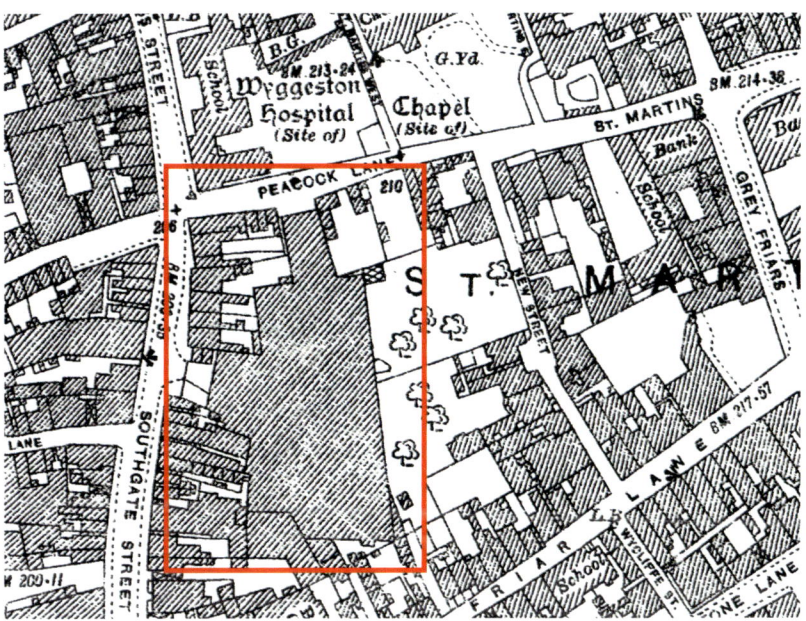

In comparison to Peacock Lane the Southgate Street entrance was a less grand affair, as can be seen from the photograph below, taken in August 1932. The enquiry office was positioned to the left of the entrance, making it easily accessible to passengers. History records that the enquiry office closed on 29 September 1979 and its work was transferred to Sandacre Street.

NEW GARAGE FOR LEICESTER.

"RED" 'BUSES' ENTERPRISE.

A new garage capable of holding 110 omnibuses was opened by the Mayor of Leicester on behalf of the Birmingham and Midland Red 'Bus Company in Southgate Street, Leicester, yesterday afternoon.

The Mayor performed the opening in the presence of a large crowd which included the majority of the members of the City Council. He gave two beats on a silver gong and the doors of the garage slid slowly open.

The new garage is built on a freehold site covering an area of 7,448 square yards. A portion of the property on Friar Lane has not been utilised, being held in reserve.

The maximum length of the garage is 350 feet, and the average width 120 feet.

Petrol tanks have been provided for the storage of 21,000 gallons of petrol. The tanks have been arranged underground and are installed in concrete vaults.

The Luncheon.

Following an inspection the Mayor (Ald. T. W. Walker) and other visitors sat down to an excellent lunch, over which Mr. R. J. Hawley, C.B.E. (managing director) presided, in the absence of Mr. C. Shirreff Hilton.

The Mayor, submitting the toast of the "Midland 'Red' Motor Services," said they owed a great deal to the Company for the way in which they had opened up the county. The omnibuses had proved a great boon to the inhabitants of the villages. The omnibuses had come to stay, and he was delighted that the "Red" Company had come to Leicester. He mentioned that Leicester had just sufficient room for a large engineering works, if the Company wished to open one.

Leicestershire Record.

Mr. Hawley, in reply, said the Company operated in 20 counties, and covered an area of nearly 10,000 square miles. They carried over 60,000,000 passengers last year, and owned between 500 and 600 vehicles, mostly single deck omnibuses with pneumatic tyres. In Leicestershire last year they ran over 3,000,000 omnibus miles and carried over 10,000,000 passengers.

The Company had grown because their motto was "public service." He thought the garage they had opened was the best of the system.

Ald. G Banton, in toasting the Chairman, spoke of the honourable understanding between the Tramways and Omnibus Company.

How the official opening ceremony was reported in the Leicester Mail, 28 June 1927.

This is the bus and coach station area at Southgate Street garage, with the part of the building fronting onto Peacock Lane in the background. It is certain that the photograph was taken in the late spring/early summer of 1930. The vehicle furthest from the camera appears to be either HA 4967 (A1057) or, more likely, HA 4987 (A1080), an SOS XL/Brush C30F saloon new in 1929. In 1930 they were converted, along with the rest of the class, to 6-cylinder MM types with new Ransomes B34F bodies. They were also re-registered into an HA 5*** sequence, so we can be sure this photo was taken before the rebuilding. Very little can be gleaned about the vehicle in the centre, apart from the fact that it is an SOS QL, new in 1928. The type had either Brush or Ransomes B37F bodies. The vehicle nearest the camera is another SOS XL, and although the registration number is not very clear, it may be that it is another from the range HA 496*. It is fitted with route boards showing that it is working the Leicester to Birmingham service.

The photographer has captured this view of the coach station at a quiet moment in 1938. All bar one of the buildings on the opposite side of Southgate Street were demolished in the 1960s when the Southgates underpass was built.

Midland Red services to Birmingham departed from the coach station for some 50 years. D5 3481 (MHA 481) is going to be the next to leave; D7 4085 (THA 85) has recently arrived back in Leicester. At this time in the mid 1950s, both vehicles were allocated to Southgate Street.

Yelloway came into being in 1931 when a consortium bought out Holt Brothers (Rochdale) Ltd. It became famous for its services from the north to London, and to the south west. WDK 952 was one of four AEC Reliance/Duple coaches new in 1960, on its way to London when photographed in the coach station early in its career. A Midland Red S15, probably bound for Coventry or Birmingham, waits in the background.

United Counties also operated a London service, the X1, originating in Nottingham and travelling via Loughborough, Leicester (Southgate Street coach station), Northampton, Newport Pagnell and Dunstable. When the M1 became available for use, journeys taking that more direct route were renumbered MX1, which option is not yet available to 121 (PNV 221), a Bristol LS5G/ECW with dual-purpose seating for 41 passengers. The children's clothes suggest this is summertime in the early 1960s, and 121 looks to be very well subscribed.

A busy scene at the coach station, in the mid-1950s, with Midland Red, Barton and Lincolnshire vehicles en route to Birmingham, Nottingham, and Grantham. The Eastern Counties half-cab Bristol, just leaving the coach station, is on an excursion to Leicester.

Long-distance stage carriage and coach services from the Southgate Street coach station reduced over time until 1980, when what was left was transferred to St Margaret's bus station. The "yard", as it then became, played host at various times to employees' cars, the two training buses, and for a few months in 1985, new Fox Cub Ford Transits. But on Sunday 10 January 1988, it was packed with Midland Fox double deck stock, including these three Fleetlines, 2911 (KUC 980P), 2900 (KUC 959P) and 2908 (KUC 246P). 2911 has recently come from the paint shop, and carries a deeper shade of yellow to that previously used.

Ten years after the photo on the left, on 30 July 1998, the yard is once again in focus, this time as the base for the Fox Cab operations. Midland Fox had moved into the taxi business in 1994, and amassed a fleet of around 25 vehicles, all Carbodies FX4s. However, it was sold to local firm Swifts in 2000. Note how the garage entrance on Southgate Street is unimpeded following the removal of the enquiry office and public conveniences.

Some idea of the interior of Southgate Street garage can be gained from these two adjacent photographs, taken around 45 years apart. CHA 1, above, was built in 1936 as an SOS REC coach, one of four experimental vehicles designed by the company's renowned chief engineer L G Wyndham Shire. It was rebuilt in 1942 (which coincidentally would become its fleet number two years later), nominally designated S2, carrying the body from sister vehicle CHA 2 adapted to a style which already bore considerable resemblance to the post-war S6 saloons. Visible to the left of 1942 are SOS SONs 1906 (CHA 530) and 2390 (GHA 309), while to the right, one of Midland Red's many FEDDs (Front Entrance Double Decker).

Mini- and midi-buses rub shoulders with deckers on 23 May 1999, by which time Southgate Street was the only remaining company garage within the Leicester boundary. Vehicles are now carrying Arriva livery - there were several changes of name and ownership between 1981 and 1997, all of which are explained in the introduction to Chapter 6. T154 AUA is a Mercedes O814D/Alexander 25-seater on demonstration duties with the company and lately employed on the X26 Mountsorrel express service; 4646 (S646 KJU) is a Volvo Olympian/Northern Counties new in August 1998. Two Mercedes L709Ds are visible in the background.

Virtually every model produced or operated by Midland Red in pre- and post-war years saw service from Southgate Street. Tilling-Stevens single- and double-deckers, Standard, Q/QL SOS's formed the bulk of the fleet in the early years and were instrumental in dispensing with the "opposition" and building up Midland Red's network of services. Later a fairly substantial fleet of MM buses and RR coaches handled many of the Leicester-based express services. By the early 1930s the Southgate Street fleet comprised entirely of single deck vehicles - particularly the IM4 and IM6 saloons of 1930-32.

The double-decker reappeared in 1932 in the shape of the REDD (Rear Entrance Double Decker) and over half of this class (HA 8004-7/13-36) were here for some time, some remaining until withdrawal. HA 8026 - later given fleet number 1410 - was seen in The Newarke.

The A.E.C. Regent (AD2 class) made an appearance after the war but more significant was the allocation of almost two-dozen D5s, which displaced the last of the REDDs. 3482 (MHA 482), photographed in Southgate Street, was there from September 1949 until withdrawn in August 1964.

Over thirty D7s were operated from Southgate Street garage. The first and last new buses of this class allocated were 4085 (THA 85) in October 1953 and 4770 (770 BHA) in October 1957. The latter bus spent all its life at SS, finally being withdrawn in August 1970. Two D7s are seen here parked in the garage in circa August 1967. 4491 (XHA 491) had been transferred from Bromsgrove in February 1966, whilst 4743 (743 BHA) was allocated from new, in March 1957. It was transferred to Hereford in July 1969.

Midland Red's final class of double deck vehicles built in quantity, the D9, had a long and historic association with the garage. The first one to be based at Southgate Street, 4881 (881 KHA), arrived in October 1960 with the final new delivery, 5430 (EHA 430D), in June 1966. This had its body completed just up the road at Loughborough by Willowbrook. 4965 (2965 HA), photographed above in Burleys Way in August 1973, was another bus to spend all its life allocated to Southgate Street, from March 1962 to April 1974.

The end of D9 operation

The historic association with the D9 referred to above relates to the fact that Southgate Street was the last Midland Red garage to operate a fleet of D9s in regular service. The end came on 31 December 1979 when the remaining six buses (5299, 5314, 5341, 5360, 5370 and 5399) were withdrawn. The last bus to return to Southgate Street was 5314, driven by Alf Bull, which is seen, above left, about to enter the garage at 6.36 pm. The other photo shows four of the last six (5341, 5370, 5314 and 5399) parked up with Daimler Fleetlines. Also note that the 'Leicester Mercury' wrongly refers to '5 buses' rather than six!

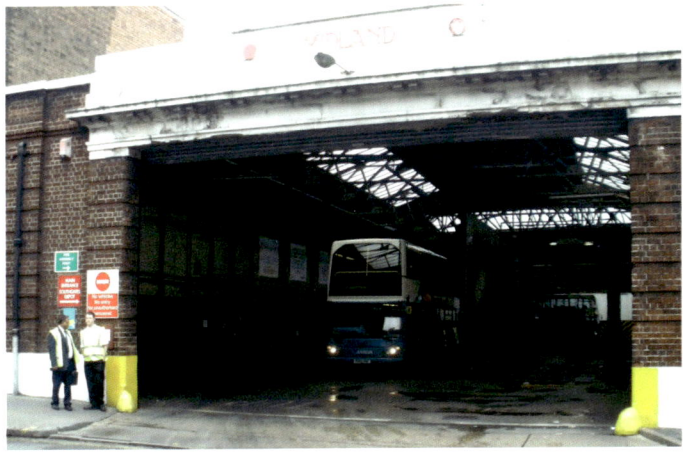

The doors of Southgate Street garage closed for the last time on Saturday 11 July 2009. We have one last glimpse inside (left), where DAF DB250/East Lancs 4726 (PN52 XBF) will be the penultimate departure, on its way to a 126 Loughborough service.

But the honour of being the very last service bus to leave went to Volvo B7TL/Wright 4008 (FJ56 OBF), below, which would form the 10.03 am service 31 from Charles Street to Oadby Grange. It is a pity the driver was not permitted to display a 31 blind when leaving the garage.

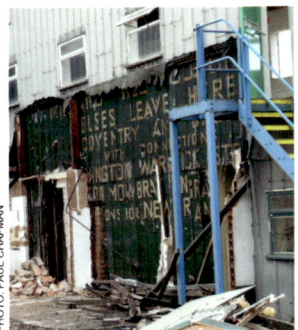

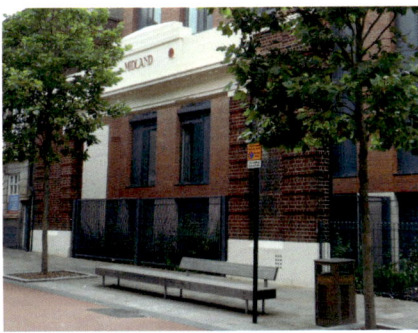

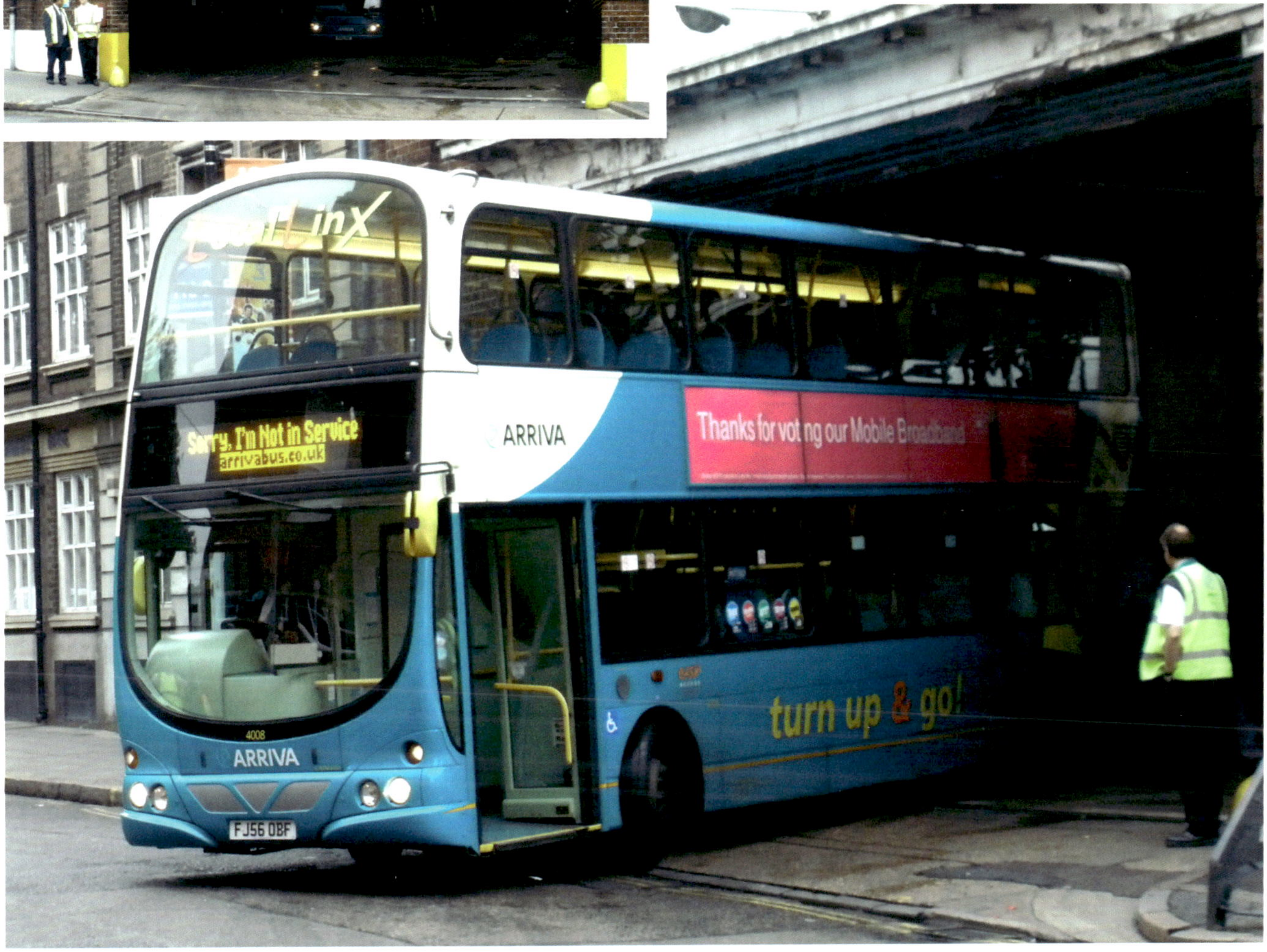

PHOTO: PAUL CHAPMAN

For a short while after closure, Southgate Street garage was used for storage purposes. But it then stood empty for several years, while all manner of replacement schemes were proposed. However, the 1.8 acre site, which included all the unbuilt land between the garage and Friar Lane which was latterly used as a staff car park, was eventually demolished and redeveloped as student housing, which is due to open in September 2017.

Visiting on 25 July 2017, the only sign that the garage ever actually stood here is the arch above the Peacock Lane entrance (top right), which the developers have incorporated as a free-standing feature in front of the flats – note there is no access via the arch any more.

ALL OTHER PHOTOS: ANDREW BARTLETT

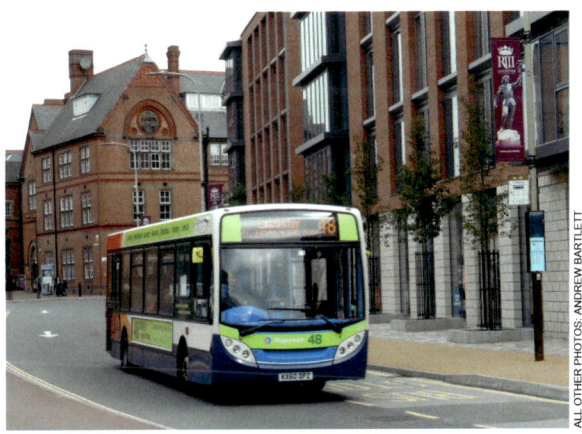

An area that was once awash with vehicles now plays host to just one service, Stagecoach Midlands 48, whose inbound journeys only traverse Southgates every 20 minutes during the day. Route-branded ADL Dart/Enviro 200 36157 (KX60 DPZ), seen on 25 July 2017, passes the bus stop which stands in more or less the same spot as in Southgates Street's glory days.

Above - Sandacre Street was very much a traditional Midland Red garage; steel framed with red brick exterior, and office accommodation on two floors, workshops and stores. This photo was taken on 14 February 1939 and shows how fortuitous the decision to build there was; the photographer is standing on what will become Platform 12 at St Margaret's bus station, of which Midland Red was a major user.

Right - Seen in the bus station is 2227 (FHA 209) an SOS FEDD (Front Entrance Double Decker). New in 1938 it originally had a Brush built 56-seat body but this was rebuilt by Hooton in circa 1950. When new 2227 would have elaborate lining out as part of its livery but by the time this rare colour photo was taken, probably in 1959, it had received all-over red. The bus was withdrawn during 1960 along with all the other remaining FEDDs. Sadly no FEDDs made it into preservation but a REDD did survive and is now at the Transport Museum Wythall.

Below - This photo of the garage dates from the mid 1950s. Stand 12 is clearly indicated!

Chapter 4

Sandacre Street Garage (1937 - 1995)
Garage Identification Code: SA

Overcrowding at Southgate Street led to the acquisition of a large corner plot bounded by Sandacre Street, Gravel Street and Mansfield Street. Sandacre Street garage, with the entrance on Mansfield Street and exits on the other two roads, had space for 70 vehicles and opened on 1 February 1937. The rented accommodation at Hastings Road, which had provided additional garage space to supplement Southgate Street from July 1932, was closed on 31 January 1937.

A photo of the exit doors onto Gravel Street. The Isetta bubble car in the bottom left hand corner was registered in early 1962 and looks pretty new. Note that it is carrying an 'L' plate. It seems an odd choice of car to learn to drive in! In the distance we can see that the Castles car showroom has been built opposite the Sandacre Street entrance.

Above, left - Parked up inside the garage in this mid 1950s photo are, from left to right, C1 3301 (KHA 301), SOS SON 1933 (CHA 557), and local independent Kemp & Shaw's Guy Arab III/Barnard 29 (FJF 90). Midland Red acquired the share capital of Kemp & Shaw in 1955 but operated the business as a subsidiary until 1959. Whilst Kemp & Shaw's vehicles were still garaged overnight in their Thurcaston Road premises for any layovers, during the daytime Sandacre garage was utilised. No. 29 would become Midland Red 4843, whilst 27 (EJF 669), above right, also on a layover in the garage, would become 4841.

D7 4402 (VHA 402) sits at the rear of the garage while sister vehicle, which appears to be 4452 (VHA 452), receives attention.

In the early 1960s Midland Red was starting to struggle to keep pace with the number of new vehicles required. Accordingly it turned to Leyland for 100 Leyland Leopard single-deckers with either Weymann or Willowbrook bodies which were designated LS18. For double-deckers an order was placed with Daimler for 50 rear-engined Fleetline chassis with Alexander bodies, the DD11. Delivered during the first half of 1963, Leicester garages received a fair number of these buses from new, including 5249 (5249 HA), above, in March 1963. It was allocated to SA along with 5265, 5266 and 5283, Southgate Street received 5248, 5262-5264, 5281, 5282 and 5292; while Wigston were the recipients of 5250, 5267-5269, 5284 and 5285. During their lifetime 5254 and 5276 also worked from SA and SS garages. 5249, 5262-5265, 5269, 5281, 5282, 5284, 5285 and 5292 remained at Leicester all their lives with the last being withdrawn in 1976.

Towards the end of their lives many of the D9s were beginning to look quite tatty. It was quite a surprise when a number of the class, including SA's four - 5299, 5362, 5370 and 5399 were given a full repaint into the latest NBC style, with the 'double-arrow' in a square box. Here we see 5399 (BHA 399C) looking as though it is ex-works in December 1978. 5370 (6370 HA) behind has still to be sent to the paint shop. The four SA D9s were all transferred to Southgate Street in February 1979.

Vehicle numbers reduced during the 1970s to such an extent that the decision was taken to close Sandacre Street garage, this event taking place in May 1980. The premises were then leased to National Car Parks (NCP), whose prominent blue sign can be seen behind 364 (GOL 364N), a Marshall bodied Leyland Leopard based at Southgate Street. It is carrying the short-lived Midland Express livery used by all the former Midland Red companies as well as United Counties, for long-distance stage carriage services.

Photos of the Mansfield Street entrance are very rare. On this occasion in July 1983, it was actually being used as an exit! At this time the garage was still in general use as a NCP car park but was being used temporarily as a coach station during the Saturday mass exodus which characterised Leicester's traditional holiday fortnight. With a full load heading for Ingoldmells, some 87 miles away, is 2654 (MLK 654L), an ex-London Transport DMS service bus.

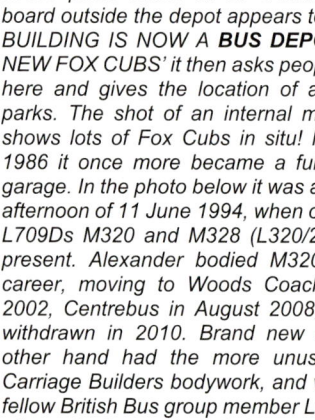

However, the minibus boom meant that space was once more at a premium, and Sandacre Street garage was reopened on 2 October 1985, initially as a storage area, as seen from the above photo taken on 27 October 1985. The board outside the depot appears to read - 'THIS BUILDING IS NOW A **BUS DEPOT** FOR THE NEW FOX CUBS' it then asks people not to park here and gives the location of alternative car parks. The shot of an internal mirror certainly shows lots of Fox Cubs in situ! From January 1986 it once more became a fully functioning garage. In the photo below it was all quiet on the afternoon of 11 June 1994, when only Mercedes L709Ds M320 and M328 (L320/28 AUT) were present. Alexander bodied M320 had a long career, moving to Woods Coaches in March 2002, Centrebus in August 2008, being finally withdrawn in 2010. Brand new M328 on the other hand had the more unusual Leicester Carriage Builders bodywork, and was moved to fellow British Bus group member Luton & District after only six months in Leicester.

The booking & enquiry office in Sandacre Street was situated on the ground floor of the garage complex, on the Gravel Street/Sandacre Street corner. The telephone information service moved from Peacock Lane to a first floor office in 1983, when the depot was in use as an NCP car park. When it reopened as the Fox Cub base, the service was moved downstairs and the Travel Centre, as it was now known, was expanded in size. It was to move again in the early 1990s, but only down the block, and a further expansion took place. Finally, on 22 September 1995, the Travel Centre closed and was relocated to Charles Street, opposite the then new Haymarket bus station; Sandacre Street garage closed the following day, with buses moving to a new base in Thurmaston.

Top right - Passing the Travel Centre in 1986, Plaxton bodied Leyland Leopard 2610 (VYM 505M) is heading for Market Harborough on express service X61. It came to Midland Red East from Cumberland in 1982.

Right - Getting a picture on Gravel Street was dependent upon there being few coaches, service buses or taxis to obscure the view. This was almost the case on 7 August 1993, when Ford Transit M466 (E955 LNR) was parked at the end of the coach bay and the northernmost depot door – in need of some TLC, it could be said – fitted into the end of the shot. M466 was new to Penniston, Melton Mowbray, a business acquired by Midland Fox in April 1988.

Below – Taken on 25 July 2017 from virtually the same spot as those early photographers is the current view of what was Sandacre Street garage. The premises, substantially altered, have for many years been used as a nightclub, painted in these unflattering, sombre black tones. Arriva DAF DB250/Wright 4769 (FJ06 ZRO) has just arrived at the stop opposite what was the Sandacre Street entrance with a 153 working from Market Bosworth.

This page contains a set of official Midland Red photos taken in November 1957, so shortly after Wigston garage was opened. The spacious docking area is shown in the above photo. Beyond the two D7s is an ex-Kemp & Shaw Guy Arab. For many years Wigston provided a centralised docking and maintenance facility for buses from surrounding garages, including the CM5 class of coaches allocated to Nuneaton garage and used on the Coventry to London motorway service. In the above right photo we expect that the large number of people in the enquiry office were in fact Midland Red office staff. We do know that it was Mrs. S. Weston behind the counter. Below is the staff canteen whilst in the bottom right hand corner we see D5 3461 (MHA 461) in the bus wash. The figure 13 on this photo was part of the artwork when it was used in Midland Red's Staff Bulletin (No. 134).

MIDLAND RED IN LEICESTER   32   WIGSTON GARAGE

Chapter 5

Wigston (Station Street) Garage (1957 - current)

Garage Identification Code: SS/WS

Once more, overcrowding elsewhere (Southgate Street and Sandacre Street on this occasion) led Midland Red to build another new garage. This time it was in Station Street, South Wigston, to the south of the city. Like Sandacre Street 20 years earlier, the garage was brick-built on steel frames and had two entrances, offices, engineering workshops and stores, with ample outdoor parking which backed onto the Leicester to Rugby railway line.

The initial allocation was 41, although the garage was capable of holding as many as 65 vehicles. It became operational on 5 October 1957.

As seen in the list below D5 3457 (MHA 457) was allocated to Wigston when the garage opened. Here it sits on the forecourt in May 1961 ready to take up a duty on Leicester local service L88 to Eyres Monsell via Saffron Lane, which was joint with Leicester City Transport. 3457 was withdrawn in July 1964.

WIGSTON GARAGE VEHICLE ALLOCATION - OCTOBER 1957

With the help of Ken Jubb, Midland Red's fleet allocation officer, it has been possible to identify 40 of the first 41 vehicles allocated to Wigston in October 1957. They were drawn from both Southgate Street and Sandacre Street fleets, and carried Southgate Street destination blinds (with the garage code SS) for the first three years. Late in 1960, Wigston (WS) blinds were supplied.

BMMO **FEDD** double deckers with Brush bodywork	2130 2135 (EHA 262/67)
BMMO **S6** saloons with Metro-Cammell bodywork	3023 3027 3043 (HHA 624/28/44)
AEC Regent II **AD2** double deckers with Brush bodywork	3100 3113 3119 3123 3124 (JHA 1/14/20/24/25)
BMMO **S8** saloon with Metro-Cammell bodywork	3276 (JHA 876)
BMMO **S9** saloon with Brush bodywork	3436 (LHA 436)
BMMO **D5** double deckers with Brush bodywork	3457 3458 3459 3460 3461 (MHA 457-61)
BMMO **D5B** double deckers with Brush bodywork	3835 3861 (NHA 835/61)
BMMO **S13** saloons with Brush bodywork	3894 3898 (OHA 894/98)
BMMO **S13** saloon with Nudd bodywork	3923 (OHA 923)
BMMO **D7** double deckers with Metro-Cammell bodywork	4085 4096 4116 4118 4120 4125 4136 4156 4158 (THA 85/96, 116/18/20/25/36/56/58)
BMMO **S14** saloons with Carlyle bodywork	4266 4283 4285 4286 4287 (UHA 266/83/85-87)
BMMO **D7** double deckers with Metro-Cammell bodywork	4397 4404 4415 4419 (VHA 397, 404/15/19)

There are clues to the identity of the 41st vehicle on Wigston's strength, but as yet no absolute proof. What is known is that virtually every garage was allocated a coach at this time, and BMMO C1 3317 (KHA 317), which had been resident at Southgate Street in March 1956, was transferred to Wigston at some point thereafter. The photo below, being another from the set taken in November 1957, certainly includes a C1 coach on the right hand side of the garage.

Here is 3457 again alongside English Electric bodied SOS SLR coach 1980 (CHA 962) at the rear of the garage. The railway can be seen in the background, although not for much longer; the line had closed on 1 January. It seems as though 1980 is still gainfully employed as a driver trainer. 3457 has obviously done a stint on the L8 – a circular route from St Margaret's bus station via Welford Road, Wigston Magna, South Wigston and Saffron Lane to The Newarke – known by Wigston drivers as "The Track".

We are still in the yard, but looking back towards the garage buildings and S13 saloon 3941 (OHA 941) stands out of service. New in May 1952, it spent almost all its working life at Digbeth, arriving in Wigston in July 1964. It was withdrawn in August 1965, and even a cursory look at its condition suggests that day is not far away (and may have already arrived), and the plentiful space available meant that Wigston had its uses as a store for withdrawn buses. The L15 was a seven-day operation which ran from Scraptoft to Enderby, although the blinds are somewhat unhelpful in this respect.

Wigston received a good number of D7s as part of its allocation, including 13 examples transferred in when the garage was opened. 4380 (VHA 380) arrived later from Southgate Street, in November 1967, and is seen here on 1 June 1968 standing in the Newarke Street (also known as York Road) bus station.

A total of 40 D9s operated from Wigston at one time or another. The first was 4884 (884 KHA), delivered new in November 1960. Legend has it that 4883 was supposed to be the first to be allocated but had an incident with a low bridge on delivery, so after repair started life at Sheepcote Street, Birmingham instead. In this photo, taken in the back yard of the garage in June 1977, there is a line-up of seven members of the class. Crew operation ceased shortly afterwards with the following transfers taking place - 5297 to Tamworth, 5341 and 5358 to SS, 5351 to SA, while 5334 and 5345 were withdrawn. These moves took place in July 1977, except for 5358 (August).

5907 (PHA 507G) was a member of the 35 strong 'S22' class and was delivered new to Wigston in September 1968. This was the final body shape produced at the company's Carlyle Works in Birmingham. This class was fitted with 45 dual-purpose seats and was the first batch of buses constructed from new for one person operation. 5907 was transferred to Leamington Spa garage in March 1980 and was then withdrawn in May 1980.

The Leyland National was first introduced to Leicester in March 1973, and seen in the yard at Wigston, 158 (HHA 158L) on the right came from Southgate Street in July 1978. Its companion, 639 (PUK 639R) arrived at Wigston from new (July 1977). Neither stayed long in the fleet however; 158 was despatched to Midland Red South in October 1981, while 639 found its way to Shrewsbury in Midland Red North territory in December 1982. The 8, or L8 was described earlier; the 7 was the reverse, or anti-clockwise, variant.

Wigston received a fair quantity of second hand double deckers including many members of the London Transport DMS class. The first DMS to receive the Midland Fox prototype livery was 2754 (GHM 764N), a 1974 Metro-Cammell bodied Daimler Fleetline CRL6. It was photographed leaving St. Margaret's Bus Station in June 1983. It was allocated to Wigston in January 1984, the same month, when, on 15th, Midland Fox was launched. It was unique in being the only DMS to carry what was to become the Midland Fox livery with Midland Red fleet names applied.

Midland Fox operated a number of schools services from Wigston depot, some reaching as far away as Market Harborough. In this photo, taken on 7 February 1996, 4151 (E701 XKR) is emerging from the depths of the depot to take an afternoon run on S291. 4151 and sister 4152, both Alexander bodied Scania N112DRBs, had arrived from Kentish Bus the previous December, but for the photographer, 4151 was the better draw as it was not painted into fleet livery for some months. The identity of the Olympian on the right is hidden by a goodly layer of winter grime.

Both Mercedes 709Ds in this view of the yard at Wigston on 30 December 2000 had only recently been transferred there, and both were in their final 12 months with the company. Reeves Burgess bodied 1339 (G301 RJA) had come from Coalville, and is helpfully displaying a "Midland Fox" blind three years after the Arriva re-naming. Behind it, M313 (L313 AUT) was an ex-Thurmaston machine still in the old red and yellow livery. The extent of some of the building that had taken place at the rear of the garage since the 1980s can be clearly seen.

At considerable risk of personal injury, Andrew was able to capture this view of the yard on 24 February 1985 from the top of a conveniently place mound of earth. From left to right, the vehicles on show were Fleetlines 6170 (SHA 870G), 2616 (LHD 304K), 2631 (MLK 631L), 2654 (MLK 654L) and 2622 (LHD 311K); 6170 had been withdrawn from Southgate Street the previous month and was the only one of the five to have begun its life with Midland Red. As for Andrew's perch, building work would soon close off this particular avenue to photographers.

On Wednesday 2 October 2002 a fire broke out at Wigston garage. It was believed to have started in the bodyshop, and residents in the nearby area had to be evacuated because of concerns that gas cylinders at the site could explode. No-one was hurt, but three Scania N113DRB double deckers were damaged beyond repair - 4156 (F156 DET) and 4164/4167 (M164/167 GRY). Two Mercedes Vario O814 minibuses, including 1123 (P123 HCH) were also affected, but were repaired and returned to service.

When Southgate Street garage closed in 2009 various services to the south of the city and around 40 vehicles were transferred to Wigston, and space for additional parking was acquired at the rear. A look inside the garage on 8 September 2012 shows one of the former Southgate Street machines, Volvo B7TL/Wright 4003 (FJ06 ZPV), a regular performer on the 31/31A Oadby routes. In the background, DAF DB250/East Lancs 4705 (Y705 XJF) was always a Wigston bus until it was transferred to Arriva Cymru in 2014.

Examples of early Arriva publicity

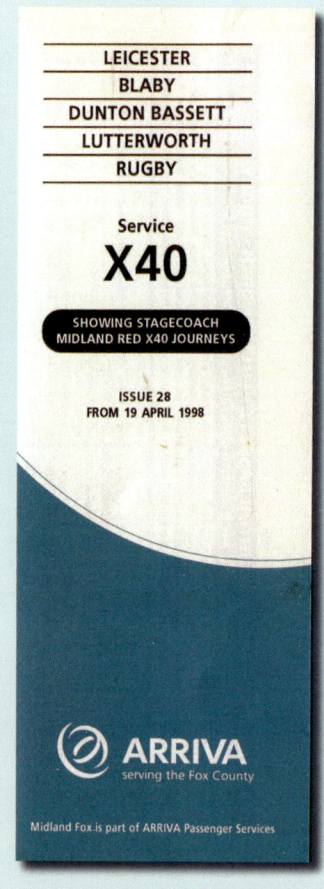

Chapter 6

Arriva Arrives - 1997

Having seen buses with different names and liveries in recent photographs, now would be a good time to explain in more detail how these changes from the Midland Red of the 1920s to 1970s came about, as Arriva reaches its 20th anniversary in Leicester and nationwide during 2017.

Midland Red had become part of the National Bus Company (NBC) on 1 January 1969. Within 18 months, it saw its bus building operations wound down. December 1973 saw the sale of Midland Red services that operated within the jurisdiction of the newly created West Midlands Passenger Transport Executive to that body. Then on 29 March 1974, the company was renamed, from BMMO to Midland Red Omnibus Co Ltd. Apart from Leicester and what was left of the Black Country operations, what remained was a largely unremunerative network. In February 1981, it was announced that Midland Red would be split into five bus operating units; North, East, South, West, and a separate local 'Express' coaching unit, with Midland Red Omnibus Co Ltd continuing as an engineering and property-holding company. So on 6 September 1981 Midland Red East came into being. However, local managers were unhappy with the name, feeling it to be contrived. They chose Midland Fox to replace it, along with a new livery of yellow and red, the colours being split diagonally a third of the way along the side of the vehicles, and 15 January 1984 was the first day of operations.

Successive Transport Acts of 1980 and 1985 paved the way for the privatisation of NBC subsidiaries, and Midland Fox was initially the subject of a management buy-out – a consortium of its own directors and those of Stevensons of Uttoxeter – in 1987. Two years later, Midland Fox was acquired by the Drawlane group (later renamed British Bus), and that is how things remained until 1986, when Cowie's came upon the scene.

Cowie's was founded in the 1930s, and became a successful car dealership in the 1960s. In the 1980s it took over Grey-Green, at that time principally a coach operator, but success in the London bus tender market and two notable purchases – Leaside and South London – when London Buses was privatised, turned it into a significant player in the bus market. It was around this time that British Bus unsuccessfully attempted a stock market listing, and Cowie's stepped in to buy the group in August 1996.

British Bus had never adopted the sort of corporate image in the way that, say, Stagecoach had, so Cowie's found itself with over 90 different brands (and brands within brands). For a year, there was no outward change, but in November 1997, vehicles in a new livery of aquamarine and stone were to appear, initially in Leicestershire on two Plaxton bodied Volvo B10Ms, as Cowie was reborn as Arriva. The name Midland Fox was gone, replaced with just the strapline "Arriva serving the Fox County", though this too would be phased out within a few years.

The second of the B10Ms, 235 (GIL 6949, originally D210 LWX) was on its way to Northampton when seen in Gravel Street, close by the former Sandacre Street depot, on 24 January 1998. It still carries an "ON HIRE To Foxhound" notice in the front windscreen.

The last new double deck buses to come to Midland Fox whilst in British Bus ownership were 20 Scania N113DRB with East Lancs bodywork, 13 of which went to Wigston, the remainder to Southgate Street. This is 4167 (M167 GRY), running "wrong way" along Bishop Street in Leicester as a result of roadworks on its normal route, Horsefair Street. 4167 was one of several vehicles to receive Leicestershire Road Safety campaign overall advertisements, in which guise it was withdrawn in October 2002 after being severely damaged in the fire at Wigston depot which is referred to on page 35.

The arrival of ten Scania L113CRL/East Lancs saloons at Southgate Street in March 1996 also heralded a startling new, dark blue livery with stylised "Urban Fox" fleetnames. Subsequent new vehicles, and some older ones too, received the scheme until it was superseded by Arriva corporate colours. Here, 2172 (N172 PUT) was loading in Narborough for the return to Leicester on its first day in service, 4 March 1996.

Midland Fox maintained a fleet of coaches for longer distance stage carriage services, private hires and National Express duties. Some carried Foxhound fleetnames and livery, and there were several variations in colours and styles over the years. Duple bodied Leyland Tiger 28 (BPR 108Y) carries a later scheme as it departs from Birmingham with an X66 Leicester service. The Foxhound name was lost under Arriva ownership, and the coaching stock dwindled until only those on National Express work were left. These were transferred to Arriva The Shires in 2010.

The small bus fleet at the time of the Cowie takeover was some 150 vehicles, most of which were Mercedes 709Ds or Iveco Daily 49.10s. There were some interesting second-or third-hand acquisitions, arguably none more so than M402 (F272 OPX). This Mercedes O811D/Robin Hood 29-seater began life with R & I Coaches of London, passing to Stevensons in January 1990 and Midland Fox in September 1994. Three months later on 21 December it was to be found in Humberstone Gate on a 53 working to Thurnby Lodge, but perhaps it was the fact that it was non-standard that saw it shipped out to Hinckley the following year, and Coalville after that. It was withdrawn in 2000.

The first new vehicles in the Arriva era were 20 Mercedes O814/Plaxton, fleet numbers M127-M146. The first nine were received in November 1997 in blue Fox Cub livery; the last of these, M135 was allocated to Thurmaston along with the December arrivals, and as these came in corporate colours, M135 was sent away for an immediate repaint. On a sunny winter's morning, 31 December 1997, M141 (R141 LNR) waits for custom in St Mary's Way, Melton Mowbray.

The first double deck vehicles of the new era emerged in March 1998 in the shape of 17 Volvo Olympians with Northern Counties bodywork. They all came in corporate livery, and reintroduced route branding for Loughborough (126/27), Braunstone (104) and, as in this case, Ibstock and Market Bosworth (152-154) on Coalville-based 4622 (R622 MNU). It was photographed in Manor Road, Desford on 4 April 1998.